PRAISE FOR

Everyday Entre 🖒 **W9-DBL-468**

"*Everyday Entrepreneur* offers a simple but effective road map anyone can use to take the fear out of following their entrepreneurial dreams."

— Monica Mehta, award-winning author of *The Entrepreneurial Instinct* and *INC Magazine* columnist.

"Fred Dawkins employs a likeable cast of characters and the simple setting of Canadian cottage country in July to convey a complex set of ideas ranging from the nature-versus-nurture debate (are entrepreneurs born or made?) to a variety of essential how-to entrepreneurship skills to specialty topics such as gender, leadership, negotiation, and team formation, as well as the important role of entrepreneurship in the global economy. His casual, easy-to-read writing style belies the critical importance of his subject matter. Not just potential entrepreneurs but also governments, big companies, and business schools in the West must adapt to the new reality of an increasingly educated and ambitious middle class in so-called developing countries and take immediate steps to reinvigorate our large population of underutilized problem-solvers in order to remain competitive and continue to enjoy increasing prosperity. As Sam would say: It is not a question of if, but rather how."

— Ajay Agrawal, Peter Munk Professor of Entrepreneurship at the University of Toronto's Rotman School of Management, founder of the Creative Destruction Lab for entrepreneurs, and co-founder of The Next 36 entrepreneurship program.

"Technology entrepreneurs all too often focus only on different ways of acquiring customers, equity value, and raising venture capital money. What is lost in the discussion is all the human issues you will face as you build your business. Fred Dawkins offers a perspective that I think is missing in the current international discussion around entrepreneurship and one that I think founders of technology companies need to consider at an early stage."

— Jesse Rodgers, director of the Creative Destruction Lab at the University of Toronto, builder of VeloCity at the University of Waterloo, and co-founder of *Tribehr.com*.

"I just finished reading [this] book and enjoyed it immensely. [Fred has] pulled together a wealth of knowledge and advice crucial to the successful entrepreneur in a highly readable fashion. It is a must-read for aspiring and seasoned entrepreneurs who are facing today's complex, volatile, and uncertain world. I especially appreciate the emphasis on thinking globally and adapting proactively. We have seen too many examples of yesterday's winner relying on old models to their detriment. It isn't easy ... but it is exciting and gratifying to create your own business and work to see it flourish. The summary at the end of the book should be bookmarked on every entrepreneur's computer."

— Dr. Sherry Cooper, chief economist for Sherry Cooper Associates, former executive VP and chief economist for BMO, and author of three books, including *The New Retirement: How it Will Change Our Future*.

"The analyses of factors dominating business and society are insightful and demonstrative. Fred Dawkins has a wonderful capacity to put things in perspective, a writing style that is captivating and his command of the English language speaks for itself. I believe this will make a great college text book since it would inspire great discussions — arguments? I'd love to be teaching from it. Also a great question and answer book for would-be entrepreneurs."

— Dr. Freeman McEwen, Dean Emeritus, University of Guelph.

"Wonderfully scribed. [The] story is easy to read, compelling, and worthy of a broad spectrum of society. As I got deeper into it, despite the undocumented postulates of Sam's theories, the story continuously got more intense while spinning off increasingly important concepts required of any entrepreneurial undertaking. Sam's ideas ring with the sounds of truth, wisdom, and familiar experiences. I loved it."

— Marvin Barnett, president, Finer Space Corporation, serial entrepreneur of over forty years.

"I worked with Fred during the negotiations of a first collective agreement for his business which was growing rapidly. His understanding of the issues and his coolness in what many would describe as high pressure moments contributed to his ultimate success and control of the situation. Before you quit your job to set up your own business or hire an accountant or do your due diligence you should read this book."

— Steven F. Wilson, partner, Mathews, Dinsdale & Clark LLP

THE ENTREPRENEURIAL EDGE

EVERYDAY
Entrepreneur
MAKING IT HAPPEN

Fred Dawkins

DUNDURN
TORONTO

Editor: Jennifer McKnight
Design: Jesse Hooper
Printer: Webcom

Library and Archives Canada Cataloguing in Publication

Dawkins, Fred, 1945-, author
    Everyday entrepreneur : making it happen / Fred Dawkins.

(Entrepreneurial edge)
Issued in print and electronic formats.
ISBN 978-1-4597-1909-5 (pbk.).-- ISBN 978-1-4597-1910-1 (pdf).--ISBN 978-1-4597-1911-8 (epub)

    1. Entrepreneurship. 2. Success in business. 3. New business enterprises. I. Title. II. Series: Entrepreneurial edge (Series)

HB615.D39 2013   658.4'21   C2013-906064-2
                                          C2013-906065-0

1   2   3   4   5   17   16   15   14   13

Canada

We acknowledge the support of the **Canada Council for the Arts** and the **Ontario Arts Council** for our publishing program. We also acknowledge the financial support of the **Government of Canada** through the **Canada Book Fund** and **Livres Canada Books**, and the **Government of Ontario** through the **Ontario Book Publishing Tax Credit** and the **Ontario Media Development Corporation**.

Care has been taken to trace the ownership of copyright material used in this book. The author and the publisher welcome any information enabling them to rectify any references or credits in subsequent editions.

J. Kirk Howard, President

The publisher is not responsible for websites or their content unless they are owned by the publisher.

Printed and bound in Canada.

VISIT US AT
Dundurn.com | *@dundurnpress* | *Facebook.com/dundurnpress* | *Pinterest.com/dundurnpress*

Dundurn
3 Church Street, Suite 500
Toronto, Ontario, Canada
M5E 1M2

Gazelle Book Services Limited
White Cross Mills
High Town, Lancaster, England
L41 4XS

Dundurn
2250 Military Road
Tonawanda, NY
U.S.A. 14150

Thanks to my wife, Karin, whose unconditional support has given me the courage to do so many things, including write this book.

To my mother, Helen C. Dawkins, who shared my love of reading and introduced me to that mutual joy with a membership to a book club when I was six.

To my father, William "Huck" Dawkins, whose passion was to ensure that his three sons received the education that he was denied.

To my father-in-law, Frank Heller, who started me on this path and gave me my first exposure to independent business.

And finally, to three people whom I've never met, Dr. Henry A. Coxe, Rudolph Heller, and Richard Muller, my grandfather and my wife's grandfathers, all of whom by genetics, osmosis, or opportunity, but especially by example, have influenced my career as an entrepreneur.

CONTENTS

ACKNOWLEDGEMENTS

It's impossible to properly acknowledge everyone that has had an impact on my career as an entrepreneur since 1969. The obvious and principal acknowledgement has to be to my wife, Karin, who has shared every bump in the road along the way. She has made so many contributions, not the least of which has been income splitting. There have been so many other influences from employees to customers to suppliers and professional advisors, all of whom have changed my perception of the business world in some way. To all of you I say thanks for the lessons learned, the challenges offered, the failures endured, and the successes enjoyed. As Sam would say, "it has to be fun," and my wild ride certainly has been that.

I do want to specifically thank my business partner and friend of the past forty five years, Ron Heller. Who would have thought any of this possible when we first agreed to go down the road of partnership? When we we're young and unproven there were many older, wiser men who mentored us through those first years, often without us noticing. Perhaps it's time to return the favour and shepherd some new players into the world of small business.

I also have to thank my brother, Don Dawkins, for sharing some of these adventures along the way. It has seldom been boring.

I would also like to thank my most perceptive business partner, who understands me the best: my daughter, Jane, with whom I've shared some great creative experiences as she developed her own spirit of entrepreneurship. Jane has taught me while I attempted to guide her. My other two children, Kris and Rob, continue to teach me as well in differing ways. All three are major factors in who I have become.

There have been many friends along the way with whom I've shared hours of conversation about business, politics, and economics. All of you have challenged me and helped mould my opinions, which are many and hopefully compelling. I would like to thank Brian Barbeau, my oldest good friend, for his presumptive role as the first one to read my new books (now up to a total of two) and Freeman McEwen, my newest good friend, for his insight and feedback. Also thanks to my friend Jill Hurst for telling me the story of the enterprising student who stole a kiss from her, all those years ago.

I could not have written this book without all of the guidance and suggestions I received from the two editors who helped me with my first book, *2020 Hindsight*, Alethea Spiridon-Hopson and Dominic Farrell. Working with a freelance editor is a terrific boost for any aspiring writer.

I am forever grateful to Patrick Boyer who was the first publisher to believe in me and was instrumental in my becoming a published author.

Finally, I would be remiss if I didn't thank Beth Bruder, vice-president of Dundurn, for suggesting I write a book on my career experiences during a meeting I had to promote my first novel. Her suggestion quickly grew into *Everyday Entrepreneur*, but I must remind you, Beth, I haven't given up on the novel — after all, *Hindsight* is *2020*.

INTRODUCTION

"The most important skill in the 21st century will be the ability to create your own job."

On March 29, 1969, my world changed dramatically. At the time, I was in the midst of year end exams during my master's year. I had just taken the first set of interviews for a position at Ryerson, teaching economics. There was no plan for me to go into business. That morning my father-in-law suffered a fatal coronary thrombosis. Five weeks later I was sitting at his desk working beside his son, engaged in a one year commitment to help my friend adjust to running the small family business. That one year agreement turned into a lifelong career as an entrepreneur, a calling for which I was meant but could easily have missed.

I believe that we all have entrepreneurial traits in varying degrees. While we revere these characteristics in those who are highly successful, many of us are denied the opportunity to use the abilities we possess either by fear and apprehension or often by outside influences and culture.

When you Google "books on entrepreneurship" the search comes up with 31,900,000 results in .22 seconds. A similar search on Amazon.com comes up with 26,470 actual books in about the same time. Do we need one more? Definitely! Entrepreneurship has never been more critical. The numbers prove that entrepreneurship retains its mystique; explaining the inexplicable offers a striking challenge. Having your own business is like winning the lottery; we all think we deserve it and we all dream of finding the winning idea, just like picking the winning ticket. Fortunately, the odds are much better and, as you'll see, they can be improved. What makes this book different? It's not written by an academic. It's not an autobiography of a business superstar. Instead it provides a view from the mainstream of entrepreneurship, the world of small business that you may hope to join.

North America has been defined by the spirit of entrepreneurship. Most of us are here because either we or our ancestors took a major risk in order to improve our day-to-day lives and to advance the future. It may not seem quite as difficult today, but new immigrants, like others before them, still take significant risks just to get here while their compatriots waver. The decision to come has combined the willingness to make major changes with taking bold action to follow an overriding desire to find something new: risk, reward, and innovation — what could be more entrepreneurial? Those who have been risk averse stayed behind and waited for the world to change. Some of us and our forefathers have made that world change to our benefit and that of many others.

Entrepreneurship must be in our DNA. We certainly recognize, celebrate, and worship success. From Edison to Jobs, we revere the extreme cases of entrepreneurial achievement. In the process, we dream of replicating the same dynamic results. The myth of becoming an entrepreneur has been closely tied to extreme risk taking, resulting in unprecedented business achievement in an area that no one else had considered. This is roughly equivalent to being called up from your high school baseball team and hitting the game-winning home run on a pinch hit in the seventh game of the World Series, in the bottom of the ninth, on an 0 and 2 pitch with two out against the best pitcher in the game. Pretty sure this has never happened in baseball, but it has in business, Facebook being the most recent example. However, we need to celebrate and encourage our small successes as well as those of the super gurus, the things that more of us have a chance to achieve. We need to celebrate effort and determination to make things happen on every scale, not just genius.

Everyday Entrepreneur is a simple story that highlights many of the key ingredients required to become an entrepreneur, someone who builds their own business or achieves the equivalent within another framework, through individual effort and initiative. With achievement comes joy and independence and sometimes, but not always, wealth. The goal of this story is to encourage those who suppress their ideas and ability because they are overwhelmed by fear that being an entrepreneur is only about the risks that you take. Maybe we can also slow down some of those gamblers who plunge ahead without good ideas and commitment, convinced that success can *only* be achieved by taking risks. It is a startling economic contradiction: too many small businesses fail through misconception and reckless mismanagement while so many good ideas die on the kitchen table from fear and indecision.

Job creation and small business are synonymous. Every politician flaunts this fact in tough economic times. Our society is facing a period where big business, big government, and big labour are combining to suppress individualism. The electronic revolution has slowed them down, but one of our most repressed resources around the world is entrepreneurship, the very catalyst that puts so many other resources to work. The extreme entrepreneurs we revere will still succeed, literally leapfrogging out of and over the masses into new big businesses. The rest of us may find it more difficult to have the independence and satisfaction of having our own business. Upward mobility may be the victim of size. This cannot be allowed to happen.

This simple story focused on promoting and understanding entrepreneurship is intended to encourage and enlighten those who will influence the future. The narrative is highlighted by real anecdotes and observations resulting from a forty-year career as an entrepreneur. Lessons are perceived through the eyes of Tim Davidson, a middle-aged manager wrestling with the dilemma of starting his own business in the midst of the Great Recession of 2009. Plagued by doubts, he has been floundering, unable to make a decision. Through a combination of fate and circumstance, Tim stumbles upon a class on entrepreneurship conducted by a mysterious character named Sam. The rest is up to Tim, as it will be up to you.

CHAPTER ONE

To Do or Not to Do?

In the summer of 2009 I was struggling with a difficult career decision. The world economy was badly shaken. Uncertainty about the future was rampant. Savings had evaporated as the markets collapsed. I wanted to make a change but I was paralyzed with fear and self-doubt. My entire work life had been spent with the same firm, developing specialized software for the transportation industry focused on increasing efficiencies and cutting costs. In spite of the economic downturn, the company was doing well, my job was secure, the benefits were above average, my savings were all in guaranteed deposit accounts; basically life was good. Yet something was missing. There was little or no sense of achievement, no excitement in anticipation of good things to come, and a long way to go to reach retirement.

For several months I had been using my spare time trying to develop specialized software focused on online training. Part of my responsibility for implementing our transportation software was to visit trucking companies and train their staff as they introduced our system. Since many of these firms had multiple locations, numerous trips were required. There seemed to be a lot of wasted effort and expense that could be avoided. Online training offered an alternative with many advantages.

I had pretty much perfected the techniques for our specific application; adding a touch of humour, some interesting online tools, and an essential interactive component that received great support from various friends whom I used to test the approach. One of my best friends, George, pushed me to go further. "Look Tim, this is great stuff. It has a million applications. Companies have been spending a fortune keeping their staff up to date on a whole range of issues and techniques. Now is *your* time — everyone is looking for cost savings and increased productivity. In-house training is such a cost effective way to improve staff performance; no travelling, lower course fees, easy access to review, and interaction among multiple locations. You can start a great business right now and be a leader. You really need to take the plunge and be your own boss. Not everybody gets the chance — especially today."

It was tempting but risky. My job was a comfort zone in the midst of a storm. My wife, Cheryl, was totally supportive. Fortunately she was a high-level civil servant with tenure. Long late-night discussions didn't resolve the issue. I was the one full of doubt. Cheryl was my advocate, and a strong one, but I was the skeptic, terrified of the consequences.

So this was the dilemma on my mind when we arrived with our three boys at my parents' cottage for a three week vacation in July. Should I take the risk? Did I have what it takes to make things work? There was no time to think about work or career change on the first day. As usual the visit started with a caustic comment from Mom who missed her family and needed to make that point before we settled in. "So great to have you all here. It's such a shame you can't come more often." Feelings of guilt followed, but not for long. My parents had sold our family home and moved into a condo several years before. The family cottage was the main physical tie to my youth. It was easy to revert and settle into the comfort zone of feeling young and carefree, if only for a few hours. That afternoon was spent water skiing, taking the kids tubing, and holding the annual jumping off the deck of the boathouse competition, with the highlight being Grampa doing it for the first time since he turned seventy. It wasn't until later that night when the kids were in bed that my Dad and I sat down on the dock to relax, rum and coke in hand.

Initially the conversation focused on the economy. Dad was a closet economist, and while he was pretty conservative with his savings, even his investments had taken a hit. I had no idea how hard of a knock, but he was troubled. "I'm afraid we're in uncharted territory, Timmy. I don't think our leaders have a clue how to fix this mess. My God, it's the biggest fall we've had since the Depression. It took twenty years and a war to get out of that one. Eighty years is a long time. We've had a pretty long run of good times without a major collapse. No one in charge has experienced anything like this. Your Granddad told me unbelievable stories of hardship about those days, but the problems are more complex today. Why we're caught in a global economy that's far more integrated than it's ever been. I have no idea where to invest."

Not exactly what I needed to hear; more gloom and doom boosting my fear and uncertainty. How countercyclical did I really want to be? Maybe I should just shelve the whole idea. Before I even mentioned what I'd been considering my Dad changed direction and started talking about a boyhood friend of mine, Terry Kelly.

"Did you know that Terry started a business up here last year? It's called 'The Cottage Deli-Café Online.' People just call it 'The Deli-Caf.' He's selling a whole range of high-end food items, specialized coffees, and he offers Internet access through in-store computers in an area where people sit and read the paper or talk — sort of Starbucks meets Whole Foods on a junior scale with Internet access — great for tourists and cottagers alike. There's a real problem getting high-speed Internet at cottages around the lake due to the rocky terrain. Being disconnected drives people crazy. His idea has gone over very well, even in the winter. There are a lot more retirees staying here year-round now. He has a wood stove in there and people flock in all year to check emails, talk politics, and buy his goodies. You should go in and see him. It took a lot of guts to jump out on his own like that, especially right now."

Sounded like another guilt trip. Maybe my father did think I needed to make a change? Or was I just oversensitive about my own indecision? Whatever the reason, the conversation about my plans would wait until later.

It was raining the next morning so I volunteered to drive into town for a few things, leaving the kids and their mother deep in a heavy game of rummy with my parents. The drive along the lake was familiar and calming. I knew every bump and turn in the road. Of course, one of the first things I noticed was a new large sign at the entrance to Town promoting "The Cottage Deli-Café Online." Terry and I had grown up on the lake together. He was a local and I was a cottager but that didn't stop us from hanging out. We were inseparable all summer. His dad ran the local marina, so Terry had a fourteen-foot Boston Whaler with a thirty-five horse power motor called the *Maryterry*, named after him and his older sister. I don't remember Mary getting much use out of it since we spent every day out on the lake in one adventure after another. It was a great life growing up. One summer we ran a little business collecting garbage by boat from all the island cottages and delivering it to the local dump. Terry recruited the customers. I seemed to do more than my share of the slugging but we did split the profits fifty/fifty. The tips were good and there were fringe benefits from the clients like free cookies and popsicles. Terry's Trash Service (the sales guy always seems to get the glory) was just one of his many ideas. I really wasn't that surprised that Terry had his own business now.

But what a vibrant, busy place it was. His Deli-Café was set up in a failed restaurant, right down on the shoreline. It had dock access for at least a dozen boats and car parking for maybe thirty vehicles. The inside was bright and cheery, a large open room with quite a number of coolers for specialty foods as well as a whole range of fresh produce. On the other side there were three computer stations and a lounge offering specialty coffees and a variety of baked goods, which could be eaten right in the lounge or bought in bulk and taken home. The cash desk was on the opposite side, alongside the row of coolers. Spread around the room were half a dozen leather arm chairs, maybe three couches, several tables with chairs apparently leftover from the restaurant, and the aforementioned wood stove, not being used in July. All the chairs were full and there were people sitting at the three computers, typing away.

I had barely stepped inside when a booming voice greeted me from behind the counter.

"Tim, it's great to see you! I wondered when you would find your way in here. Welcome to the 'Deli-Caf.' Take a seat; I'll be with you in a minute. It's fantastic that you came by. C'mon now, Mr. Harris, you've been here all morning. Let Timmy have that seat so I can talk to him."

I recognized Mr. Harris as a crabby old islander who had given Terry and me a rough time when we collected his garbage twenty years before. Not likely that he would co-operate. However, he quickly jumped up to give me his seat, nodding at me with a knowing smile as he left with two bags of Terry's specialties in hand. As I was sitting there I noticed a bulletin board with various postings of items and services for sale. This was probably a great place to get some exposure. While I was scanning the various items one in particular caught my interest. The message was simple enough: "Free Lessons in Entrepreneurship — call 555-2626." My first thought was a cynical: "wouldn't it be nice if it was that easy." The next impulse was to rip off one of the tabs with the phone number, which I did. Then just when I was going to throw it away, an arm wrapped around my shoulder and

Terry's familiar voice said, "Hold onto that, those lessons are the best thing that ever happened to me. Call today and tell Sam that Terry Kelly made you call. I don't know what you're up to Timmy, but if you ever want to strike out on your own make that call."

CHAPTER TWO

An Unusual Proposition

Terry and I didn't have much time to talk that day. He was far too busy. His venture into free enterprise seemed to be a roaring success. Little doubt about that from what I could see. There was a line up at the cash register the entire time I was there. What an atmosphere; cheery conversation, great products, the pricing was on the high side but no one seemed to be concerned. Pretty basic concept, simple actually, almost anyone could see the need. Or could they? Most people would have predicted certain failure.

After picking up a specialty blend of Turkish coffee and a dozen fresh Chelsea buns I started to leave. As busy was he was, Terry noticed and literally ran over to say goodbye. My friend seemed to have a good handle on everything whirling around him.

"Seriously, Tim, did you take that phone number? Sam can make a real difference for you, if you open your mind to his ideas."

I reached out and shook his hand, then pulled him into an overdue man hug, glad to see his smiling face and his obvious enjoyment of what he was doing.

"Let me think about it. I'm here for three weeks. I'll be in to see you in a couple of days."

Terry didn't hesitate. "Call him Tim, you won't be sorry. Trust me."

Then he rushed back into the fray, a happy business owner in the midst of obvious joy.

As I drove away, the tab with the telephone number was still in the palm of my hand. All the way back I debated how Terry had made his simple plan work so well. What made some ideas flourish while others floundered? Could I pull my plan off the way my friend had? Back at the cottage the rain continued to pour down so the rest of the family was in the midst of a high-stakes game of Monopoly. My father was busily buying hotels, intent on bankrupting his grandchildren. No irony there. No one seemed to take much notice of what I was doing, at least not after I presented them with the warm Chelsea.

After a walk in the rain to clear my mind, I settled into a comfortable chair intent on reading a book in the quiet confines of the sleeping cabin. Terry's comments kept going through my mind. Could these lessons really help? Why not check this thing out? Maybe the experience would help me decide what to do. After picking up the phone several times only to set it down again, I finally dialed the number.

It rang three times, each one prompting me to hang up, but before I could, a firm voice answered. It was clearly that of an older man.

"I assume you're calling about the lessons. I have one opening left. What's your name?"

This was ludicrous. How was some old retiree in cottage country going to help me? I was about to hang up for sure when the voice continued.

"First free lesson, indecision leads to bad decisions. So what's your name?"

This time I answered. The presence at the other end of the line demanded it.

"Tim, Sir. Actually, Terry Kelly told me to call. He says your lessons are the best thing that ever happened to him. Terry and I have been friends for years. Can you tell me about the lessons?"

There was no hesitation at the other end.

"Terry's reference is all I need. You are in the class. There will be three of you. There are always three. There is no charge. The lessons take two hours every day for two weeks and it has to be every day except Sunday. If you can't make all twelve, tell me now and don't even start. Is that clear?"

There was no pause allowing for an answer.

"So that's about it. Be at the public school in town every day at three o'clock in the afternoon. You can call me Sam. See you tomorrow."

And then he hung up, leaving me with a quiet sense of comfort, a feeling of confidence and ease. It felt good to be accepted, although I wasn't quite sure why. After all, who was this Sam who had me so easily under his thumb in a two-minute phone conversation?

CHAPTER THREE

The First Impression

One last midnight discussion with Cheryl cleared the way to go ahead. If I was willing to give up part of my holiday, she could handle the kids and my parents for three or so hours a day, *but* at the end of the course I had to make a decision.

It didn't seem wise to be late. So the next afternoon I showed up 2:40, hoping to size things up before we got started. I was the first one there and assumed that the school was locked. Out in the school yard I could see a teenager with blond hair in the distance dressed in a pair of white shorts and a green T-shirt. He appeared to be trying to chip plastic golf balls through the basketball net. He was actually fairly good at it. Kids could always invent new games to amuse themselves but it was nice to see one physically active instead of playing video games on the computer.

Soon enough a second would-be entrepreneur arrived. She was not what I had expected. An attractive woman, about my age, walked up to the door, looked inside, and then reluctantly walked over to me.

"Are you by any chance Sam?"

This made me chuckle out loud, which only added to her discomfort.

"I'm pretty sure that Sam is both older and wiser than I am. No, I'm Tim, one of the three rookies today. Not sure at all I have the right stuff. How about you, are you one of the three as well?"

She almost squirmed at the comment, looking around for some other distraction, but then she smiled.

"I'm Grace, definitely one of the three trainees. Embarrassing isn't it? Adults like us looking for courage and vindication to do something we want."

That was exactly it. I needed someone to tell me that my idea was all right, someone to tell me to go for it.

"Hardly the sign of a pair of compulsive risk takers is it?"

Just then the third candidate arrived. A young man in his early twenties walked right past the two of us, up to the door, opened it, and went inside. We followed closely behind, feeling foolish that neither of us had actually tried the door. Our third was prancing around the classroom, talking loudly on his cell-phone. There was a sign on the blackboard that simply read "Entrepreneurship." The three of us had barely entered the room when I heard a familiar voice behind us.

"I wondered how long it would take before one of you tried the door. So was it Mike on the phone or Tim? I could see it wasn't Grace."

With that one simple statement we had all been introduced quite efficiently. It was clear who was who and there was no doubt about who was in charge.

Turning around, I faced an older man, fairly tall, unshaven, wearing a scruffy pair of white denim shorts and a green T-shirt decorated with an image of a cup and the words "Half Full." His hair was a mix of blond and gray. There was a golf club in his hand but he was anything but a teenager looking to invent a game. He had looked pretty agile out in the yard but he limped slightly as he walked to the front of the room, ample evidence that things are not always what they seem. What didn't seem possible was that this apparition before us could help resolve my issues. Sam was hardly a picture of worldly success — in fact, he was the antithesis, the embodiment of an aging hippie who had no evident interest in success.

Grace looked at me as if to say "let's give him a chance," while Mike just jumped in with both feet.

"I'm Mike. I don't have time to waste. That's why I opened the door. Can we get started?"

There was a knowing smirk on Sam's face.

"We can, but just one point if we're going to do this. You have to be here every day. No matter how you feel about what we discuss. If any of you miss just once, that's the end for all of you — don't come back. This session will be over. Is that clear?"

All three of us nodded in agreement. We would show up no matter what. It would be a recurring theme, so it wasn't surprising that after that first class, over a coffee at the Deli-Caf, the three of us unanimously dubbed him "The Everyday Entrepreneur."

That first day established the pattern for the next two weeks. Sam liked to ramble on, weaving anecdotes and questions, leading us to conclusions that we thought were our own. Mike was like the kid you always hated in class — the one that always had an answer, seldom *the* answer, but at least one that he had to give because he *knew* it was right. The kid who waved his handed relentlessly to get the teacher's attention and yet the teacher hardly seemed to notice. Sitting still at his desk was not in his playbook. Grace was the opposite. She never volunteered an answer, but when she had to give one, her ideas were smart, well thought out, and thought provoking. As for me, I was somewhere in between — willing to speak up but not in a rush to do it and not as insightful as Grace.

Before he started, Sam made one thing very clear.

"We are not here to discuss technique. If you want to learn how to write a business plan, or how to market products or manage your time there are thousands of books and courses that can help you. I'm here to share my experiences and help you understand the approach and philosophy of an entrepreneur.

My goal is to bring out abilities that you have but don't recognize or that you underestimate. These two weeks are about finding yourself and a different approach to life."

Then Sam got us started with an obvious question.

"So what made you call me?"

Mike didn't hesitate, blurting out his first thought, which soon became a pattern.

"They say you made a lot of money. That's what I want; success and the money that goes it with it. I want to know how."

Sam continued looking first at me and then at Grace.

"Is that why you're here Grace? Is it for money?"

Grace squirmed as she had before.

"No, Sir. I have an idea, a plan, and I really want to try it. I just can't let it go but I don't want to fail. That would be worse than not trying. I couldn't bear to fail."

It took a while but Sam eventually drew the idea out of Grace. She was an avid knitter and wanted to start first one store and then a small chain of stores that she planned on calling "Blending a Good Yarn." She explained that her idea for the stores was based on the fact that knitting was coming back into vogue but many women needed to be helped along the way.

"Skills that used to be passed from one generation to another have generally been lost, at least to many of us. Blending a Good Yarn will sell all the materials needed but the real attraction will be the classes, lessons, and group projects that will be shared, recreating the social side of knitting groups that has been lost. There's an important social aspect to this but there's also a practical side. In the face of economic downturn home crafts generally flourish. We'll be mixing our own yarns in several ways, through conversation *and* demonstration. There'll be a computer corner for research and I intend to start a blog. All of which creates opportunity for the stores to make sales and generate profits. I love the idea but I've studied it forward and backwards to try and make sure it's viable. My goal is to start enough stores to prove the concept has merit and then sell the business to a national brand. Maybe I'm naïve?"

Sam didn't comment but turned to Mike and me. After quite a few questions showing a surprising knowledge of current technology, he had dragged out my ideas regarding online training courses. Of course, he didn't comment on this concept either, other than to say "very interesting," which made me giggle out loud thinking of reruns of the old "Laugh In" show that I watched with my dad when I was a kid.

Mike had no specific idea — he just wanted to learn how to become an entrepreneur after which he would make his plan. There was no sense speculating until he learned how.

Sam did not react to Mike's simplistic reasoning, nor did he seem at all surprised by the cavalier attitude, but it did lead him to make his first interesting comment on entrepreneurship.

"You know, one of my good friends, quite a successful innovator, once said, 'it's never been about the money. It's all about the idea and the challenge. Money is just the way you keep score.'"

Grace looked over and smiled at me. Was this part of the vindication she needed?

Mike was not deterred by this at all.

"Sam, I hear you had a lot of success. What's the biggest reward you got out of being an entrepreneur? You must have made millions."

Sam muttered something under his breath to the effect: "It always takes three. It always takes three," before he answered in a louder voice.

"Mike the money comes with the territory — it has never been the goal. The rewards are the countries I've seen, the people I've met, the things I've done, the independence gained, and the friends that I've made. Money is the medium of exchange, a by-product of success and a way to measure it, not a reward."

Mike gave Sam his most knowing look as he chuckled to Grace — he wasn't buying it.

"Yeah, sure Sam. No one ever does it for the money."

I had to admit it wasn't the money for me — maybe the challenge, maybe the freedom, but not the money. Sam was right, the money would be confirmation not the goal. Grace didn't react at all. Then Sam abruptly dismissed us — clearly avoiding further discussion.

"That's it for today. Go and give Terry some business. Same time tomorrow. Make sure you're here. You have one assignment. Each of you should bring in a list of six words that you feel best describe an entrepreneur."

Of course, Terry was waiting for us at the Deli- Caf. He would be every afternoon, eager to see our reactions and changing attitudes. He was almost gleeful when we nicknamed Sam "The Everyday Entrepreneur," nodding his head in agreement as we apparently did the predictable. But he was almost rolling on the floor with laughter at Mike's antics preaching the virtues of money as the real mark of a successful entrepreneur.

When I got home that evening, I started my list of "The Canons of Sam," or as I simply labelled it later: "Sam Says." It became a nightly ritual. As my grandfather loved to say about his overactive grandchildren, we were all full of "piss and vinegar" that first day. Somehow, and in different ways, Sam had managed to stir all of our emotions. Maybe Terry was right.

CHAPTER FOUR

Born or Made?

The next session got off to a quick start. We were hardly settled into our chairs before Sam asked for our lists, intending to read each one out loud without commenting.

Eager and confident, Mike went first, reading his own before Sam could reach him as he paced impatiently across the front of the room. His list was not altogether surprising and included:

"Rich, Gambler, Powerful, Successful, Fearless, Ruthless."

Sam was annoyed but didn't flinch, quickly grabbing Mike's list, before flipping it over to read the one submitted by Grace. He actually smiled as he read hers aloud:

"Innovative, Problem solver, Leader, Perceptive, Determined, Resilient."

Once again, no comment — just a quick flick of the wrist and a scan of mine before reading without the smile:

"Risk taker, Inventor, Trail-Blazer, Independent, Voyeur, Ambitious."

There was no doubt which one he preferred, yet there was no visible distinction in his reaction to those prepared by Mike or myself. Personally I thought Mike's was pretty shallow, but Sam didn't seem to mind.

"We'll see how you feel about these lists when we finish at the end of next week. Let's get started. So tell me about entrepreneurs — are they born or made?"

Mike was off and running. "No doubt we're born. It's in our genes. It's inevitable. You can encourage entrepreneurship but you can't teach it."

All the rest of us burst out laughing at his certainty. I was laughing because he had moved himself into the elite, but Grace made a different point.

"Why are we here then? If this whole mystic talent is so natural why are we trying to find it?"

Mike was not remotely fazed. He was a walking contradiction who lacked confidence but spoke with conviction.

"Oh, you can learn about it, but if you don't have it in you it won't matter."

It wasn't that obvious to me. Besides, I was much more interested in Sam's perspective. Mike was becoming irritating and predictable. Fortunately, Sam resumed control over the discussion.

"Let me tell you a few stories about a successful friend and some of my own experiences. Maybe that will help you decide. One of my best friends, Peter, a former business partner, has enjoyed some of the most dynamic business successes that I have seen up close. Peter is a stereotypical entrepreneur, never happy without a new project and never satisfied with the current one. By the way, I don't believe in stereotypes. They tend to be trite oversimplifications, when in reality there is no formula. There are many different types of entrepreneurs. Professional golfers are a good comparison — no two golfers have identical swing patterns, each has their own swing characteristics, none of which is perfect. The one with the most classic swing often fails to win consistently. The best golfers, no matter what their swing pattern, all come through the ball properly right at impact. It doesn't matter how they get there, but they must be square at impact. Just like golf swings, there are inevitably many different paths to success.

My advice is meant for entrepreneurs of all stripes, from the computing genius to the house cleaner. That's not today's topic, but you do need to know that there are many ways to get results and many different results to get, all with some common essential qualities. We're looking for those common bonds. Back to Peter.

"Peter loved to recite two stories that his mother told him about his boyhood, both suggesting his path was predestined. The first happened when he was five years old and managed to talk his parents into an allowance because his older brother and sister were both receiving one. That's pretty common. Anyway, he started receiving his own in September and saved faithfully to buy all of his family Christmas presents, which he did. After Christmas he had three dollars left and his mother took him to the bank to open an account. A week later, on the way home from school this rather small boy ventured into the bank, which in those days had quite high counters. An older lady, or at least one that seemed quite old to him, leaned over and said, 'What can I do for you young man?'

"Apparently my friend was not intimidated whatsoever and boldly made his request.

"'I've come in for one of your calendars.'

"The lady, who was no doubt much younger than he thought and was probably enjoying the exchange, looked down quite seriously over the raised counter before saying: 'I'm sorry sir, the calendars are just for customers.'

"To which my friend Peter replied in a very calm voice: 'I am a customer, and if you don't give me a calendar I'm taking my money out of your bank!'"

We all burst out laughing at this point in full appreciation of the youthful negotiator who would not be intimidated.

"Apparently the bank teller called Peter's mother to tell her the story after sending him on his way with not one but two calendars. The second story that Peter liked to share, usually after an encouraging response to the first one, happened the same fall in early November when he was five. Peter and his friend from next door were playing cars outside when Peter decided he needed to build a bridge in the sandbox. To do that he needed some water. When he went inside his mother absolutely refused to give him any, since it was far too cold outside to play with water. She had hardly returned to the kitchen when she heard a knock at the door. It was the boy from next door very agitated. 'Mrs. Webster, Mrs. Webster. Pete is peeing in the sandbox.' Needless to say, the bridge was built. So there you have it, to this day, my friend Peter is a formidable negotiator and has always been one of the most determined individuals any of us are likely to meet. So do you all agree that his early creativity helps make the case for entrepreneurs being born?" Mike was all smiles. Grace and I were more concerned. My mother never told stories like that about me.

Sam noticed the unbridled joy on Mike's face as he searched his memory for childhood stories that would vindicate his birthright into the entrepreneurial brotherhood. Sam waited, then smiled as he recognized a flicker of doubt in Mike's eyes; only then did he continue.

"Let me tell you a different story, one from my own experience. In 1987 South Korea was becoming a challenging factor in a number of industries, offering serious competition to North American factories. The prevailing logic was that all the Koreans had going for them was cheap labour, which wouldn't be enough to sustain their initial market penetration. That mindset hurt the west for a long while before we understood the real threats inherent in a global economy. Underestimating the competition is a reckless and unnecessary risk. Nothing lasts forever.

"Anyway, a business friend and I decided to go to Korea and see for ourselves. We found a country in a state of dynamic change with many contrasts. From the first day we saw so many contradictions. On one hand, we visited a primitive old factory in the demilitarized zone with very little equipment and antiquated methods that might have been common during the early days of the Industrial Revolution, perhaps in 1850. That was in the morning. The same afternoon we visited several new factories that were better equipped than anything we had at home.

"Regardless, everywhere the people were fabulous and their attitude was a revelation. In that first humble structure we had to share coffee in a rundown office because we were the first white visitors to ever come to their premises. This was just twenty-two years ago. The people were so excited, it was heart-warming. Initially we felt sorry for them, deceived by wishful thinking and relieved that there was no threat there. But shortly we saw countless new and updated plants in the leather and apparel industries that were more modern and current than those we had left behind. Our sympathies changed rather abruptly. North America was not ahead in all areas. A competitive maelstrom was brewing. Remember, only thirty years before Korea had been an agrarian society coming off years of Japanese occupation followed by what was a bitter and destructive civil war. The constant threat of that war resuming was evident everywhere and remains a constant of Korean life. However, in 1987 the country was on the rise and excited about the prospect of international recognition with the Seoul Olympics one short year away. National pride was visible everywhere you looked.

"In those days the typical Korean office was set up with a large desk for the president or CEO at one side of the room, usually sitting on a raised platform. Generally right in front of his desk there was a large coffee table with two couches on either side running parallel away from the large desk. The company president would often come down from his raised desk, sit in the couch on one side while his guests sat on the other and coffee was served. At one office we visited late in the trip, my friend was interested in the products while I was mainly a bystander, sitting beside him on the couch sipping my coffee, lulled into semi-consciousness by jet lag. After every question that my friend asked, the Korean owner answered enthusiastically with a heavily accented 'Yes! Yes! Yes!'

"It didn't matter what the question was — the answer was always the same. After several such exchanges, while still looking directly at the owner, my friend said, 'He doesn't understand a single word that I am saying,' to which the Korean gentleman responded, 'Yes! Yes! Yes!'"

While we couldn't help but laugh, Sam quickly subdued us.

"Of course, I laughed at the time, just like you. I couldn't help myself. The Korean owner even joined in. Still, this seemingly funny story indicates how serious and determined the Koreans were to succeed during this period. The question in their minds was never *if* things could be done, but rather *how* they would be done. To me this is one of the definitive attributes of an entrepreneur — any assessment of a challenging issue jumps almost immediately to 'how' things will be done skipping over the doubt and indecision inherent in evaluating 'if' they can be done. This is a powerful force for achievement.

"What we saw on that trip was astounding. A country of poor farmers was in the midst of becoming an industrial power in barely one generation through an aggressive national industrial policy and through a very rigid commitment to education. Every hotel room had a printed version of the government policy focused on industrialization. Students willingly worked long days and nights with confidence that education would provide opportunity. It reminded me of the determination we westerners showed following the setback of the Great Depression. So this brings us back to my original question: are entrepreneurs born or made?"

None of us wanted to speak first. I was imagining Sam sipping the coffee in the rundown factory up near the North Korea border and I was jealous. I could only wish for that type of experience. Yet the story was encouraging. If the Koreans could do it, why couldn't I? For once I spoke up.

"It seems pretty clear that entrepreneurial behaviour can be developed and certainly nourished. Maybe we all have some elements of an entrepreneur inside us that need to be drawn out. Maybe our inner entrepreneur is like our social skills that come out early for some of us but later in others and never for some. Maybe we've been confusing entrepreneurship with super success? If the Koreans could learn it why can't we?"

Sam was beaming at my comment. Grace was smiling too. Mike seemed relieved, his dreams of financial conquests revived; no longer dashed by the realization that he might not have the right genes. And that was the end of the day. Sam chose my response as the perfect point to end the discussion which made me feel great. Again the two hours had flown by. The three of us headed off to the Deli-Caf where Terry was waiting, our dreams of independence still intact.

CHAPTER FIVE

The Daily Recap

Late afternoon was a good time of day to visit the Deli-Caf. The morning was peak time when everyone wanted a coffee, conversation, and the chance to surf the net, not to mention a fresh Danish or muffin. This was a meeting place, not a dining room, a casual relaxed atmosphere, a modern version of the cafes of Vienna. By the end of the afternoon things had dwindled and Terry usually closed up shop at five. For those two weeks in the summer of 2009, he made an exception. He was always waiting for us with some semi-stale baking and freshly brewed coffee. At first I thought he was doing it just for me, for old time's sake and the chance to encourage an old friend; apparently not. Sam inevitably closed out the day by pointing us towards the Deli-Caf but he never joined us. As for Terry, he was like a cheerleader who had missed an away game — full of encouragement and desperate for details.

"Well, Tim, how did it go today? Was this the Korean trip day? That's a real eye opener don't you think? It really slayed me how a country could recover so fast from such a long period of outside dominance and destruction and become an economic powerhouse. Sometimes we forget about what's going on in the rest of the world. Kind of frightening, though. It makes you realize how hard we have to work to stay on top."

Grace nodded in agreement. She was sipping her tea, preferring that to coffee.

"Maybe that's a business lesson as well as a personal one. It's important to understand the competition. We've sort of had it our way for quite a while in the west. Now with all this globalization, things change much faster and the competition comes from every direction, fast and furious."

I had thought about that a fair amount. Working with the transportation industry was an eye opener. We had a defensible niche. Factories were closing all around us but trucking was booming. Distribution was essential no matter where products were made or for that matter grown. Part of our success as software providers related to our impact on efficiency. Logistics, the planning and the flow of goods around the world, had never been more critical. It was one of the reasons that I liked the industry I was in. Being secure gave me the confidence to add my opinion.

"It's a big part of assessing your future. What products and services can we do better here than anyone else OR what products and services can only be done locally? It's good for you, Grace — people still want to create things. They want the satisfaction of making products, but we can't do mass production of a lot of things here, at least not right now. I think your shops will be a big hit."

Mike was busily chomping away on his second Danish. He always lost interest when we talked about our ideas. He had no software background and could have cared less about knitting or any other female activity. Grace was a bit pensive and then she turned to Terry with a question.

"They say that imitation is flattering. Would you be angry if I brought some elements of the Deli-Caf into my Good Yarn idea? I think I should expand my computer set up, establish a list of favourite knitting sites, and start following some other blogs, which should be a real plus. The whole idea of a conversation area with tea and coffee to discuss patterns and techniques really appeals to me. Of course, I'm doing it in the city, not close to here."

Terry was totally supportive.

"Even if you were doing it here, you're hitting a different market, and probably a pretty good one. I can help you if you like — put you in touch with some key suppliers. You have to really think out your layout. The conversation, the coffee, and the computer are all market capture techniques but your products and services have to be up front and worthwhile or you won't make any money and the attraction will fade in a hurry."

At that point Mike got up and left.

"Thanks for the coffee and Danish, Terry. See you guys tomorrow."

At least he had the decency to say thank you. The rest of the time was filled with an animated conversation between the two innovative shop keepers. It was fun to watch.

"Have you ever thought about putting wool into a corner of the Deli-Caf? A lot of people knit at the cottage and there's nowhere close by to get patterns or supplies. Maybe we could work together. I have to get a website and I could even do some classes for you when I'm up at the cottage."

Terry was always looking for new angles.

"That would be great. I have this area in the back that I've been trying to decide how to use. Maybe I could run different classes in it all summer. Maybe two weeks of knitting. I know an artist who would teach water colours. I was even thinking of a writing group as well as a discussion group focused on politics. There are a ton of retirees here for six months looking for activities. There's a wealth of talent around here just waiting for encouragement. Of course it wouldn't hurt the business either. It would keep people coming in for a longer season and buying while they're here."

As I listened I couldn't help but think that I was watching entrepreneurship at work. The ideas were flowing, the enthusiasm was building, and snap decisions were in the air. The most important thing that I realized was that it was fun. Then I had an idea of my own.

"It seems like both of you could tie into my program of web-based seminars. Grace, you could perfect some of your knitting courses and become my online teacher for handcrafts. You could also offer some interactive online courses taught by others conducted for groups at your stores. Terry, you could use that back room to run online courses in a whole range of areas. You don't have to have instructors here."

And so it went on for another hour, a game of idea ping pong. The common bonds seemed endless and the ideas that continued to flow were exhilarating. Some of the ideas were ridiculous, making us laugh, perhaps too easily. Some would never happen or even be tried but some of them were all right. I had never had this much fun at my job and I had never been this creative in my thinking! Maybe I was starting to free up my inner entrepreneur.

That night the list grew by several statements. Mr. Everyday was scoring points.

CHAPTER SIX

Doing the Unlikeable

Technically there was no preparation required for the sessions. Sam seemed to be pretty much winging it, although Terry seemed to have a feel for what we were doing day by day. Regardless, the ideas that Sam was presenting and the responses that he managed to draw out of us were consuming me. My outlook was changing. Cynicism was on the wane. Doubt was in decline. Optimism was at least on the horizon. Maybe this mystical entrepreneurship, as much as anything, was a way of thinking — maybe a life philosophy that could be acquired after all. Sleep was elusive during those two weeks, too much to consider, an active mind overriding the need for sleep. Cheryl was pleased with my enthusiasm, less charmed by my relentless conversation after midnight.

Fortunately I had most of the day at the cottage, so the family holiday was in full swing. Every morning started early, filled by driving the boat for water skiing and tubing for my own kids and half the shoreline. Every evening revolved around cards and board games. Family rules didn't allow television at the cottage. All of this made the days and nights fly by and the stress of making a decision about my business future flow away. In fact, the weight of the decision had been lifted, at least for the moment.

Our next meeting started outside. Sam insisted that we all try his little exercise, attempting to chip plastic golf balls through the basketball net. Through a storm of protests led by Grace, who had never even held a golf club, Sam persisted. "Don't you remember anything we discussed yesterday? What is the mantra of an entrepreneur?" With just the slightest hesitation we responded in unison: "The question is never 'if' we can do it, but rather 'how' we will do it."

After half an hour of lessons from Sam and a little practice, all of us were able to chip six out of ten shots through the net. In fact, Sam wouldn't let us stop until we all did that at least once.

"Now remember, every time you face a new challenge think about how fast you learned to chip baskets, something you had no interest in doing and no idea how to go about, but you had to get it done to move ahead."

And who do you think was the last one to accomplish the six-out-of-ten requirement? Well it wasn't Grace. It was actually Mike, and he played golf regularly. The reason he was last? For Mike the challenge was a no-brainer, so he didn't listen to Sam. Just like the typical little boy blurting "Let me! Let me!" he grabbed the club without any thought or plan and flailed away. It was only when Grace did it first that he took the time to study the challenge.

That reinforced Sam's message for me. The whole idea was to find a way — not to know the way or make rash assumptions and definitely not to guess. Determination is the essential starting point, the drive behind the solution, but it isn't a replacement for study and analysis. I'm not sure that Mike will ever get it, but I still remind myself often of the second part of the message — face the things that must be done, especially those I prefer to ignore and find a way. There always is one.

The rest of the afternoon was filled with more anecdotes from Sam.

"My friend Bob had one of the most diverse careers of anyone I know. When Bob tried to sell his factory to move to a newer larger facility, he was having trouble getting anyone interested in an older building. Before I knew it Bob had sandblasted the painted brick, cleaned the concrete floors, recruited a broad range of artists, and opened what became a successful artisan's gallery, giving Bob both pleasure and an income stream. Another problem solved and yet another business for Bob. The fact that the building rose significantly in value before he finally sold it didn't hurt either.

"When Bob moved on to land development around 1990, he decided to get his real estate license. After taking his first course of several, Bob came to see me to discuss what he had learned so far.

"'Sam, did you realize that every agent legally works for the seller? Nobody understands that. The agents are legally required to tell the seller everything they learn from the potential buyer. When you establish a relationship with a realtor who takes you to see a property, your realtor legally works for the seller, not you. There's a different business here.'

"Before I knew it Bob had started his own agency called Buyer Beware. His agency worked exclusively for purchasers, much more common now than it was twenty years ago. Within five years he had franchised his new idea across the country. There are more buyer agencies now, but Bob saw the opportunity early.

"Later, after Bob retired, he decided to write a book. When he realized how difficult it was for an unknown to get published he decided to do something about it. Soon enough he started his own publishing house, which he called 'First Timers,' focused on giving new authors a platform. In the past three years he has published over one hundred books and the company is in the black with a product entirely from unknown authors that no one else wanted. Another void in the marketplace has been filled, plus Bob has acquired a whole stable of prolific writers who are loyal.

"Bob has quite a reputation. Some people think he's just plain lucky — the kind of fellow who falls into a barrel of manure and comes out smelling like a rose. So does Bob's story tell us anything about being an entrepreneur or has he just been lucky?"

As usual Mike thought he was way ahead on this one, but he was actually a step or two behind, as he blurted out: "When you concentrate on 'how' rather than 'if' you can make a lot of money."

Sam shook his head, "No, Mike that was yesterday's discussion, and forget about the money. This is about a different question all together. Sure, the 'how' comes into play in Bob's story, but there is another question that Bob was constantly asking."

Grace and I just looked at each other for a moment. Then a smile flashed across her face and she spoke up. "The other question is 'what?' I'm sure that's it, isn't it Sam? Every story you told about Bob revolved around opportunity. Bob was always looking for 'what' he might do. Once he saw the possibilities he moved on to 'how.' Is that it?"

Sam was pleased. "You're right, Grace, and faster than most. Bob still sees opportunity everywhere he looks. Most people think of entrepreneurs as 'idea' men or women. But opportunities are not the mirror image of ideas. Translating ideas into action requires much more than dreaming up possibilities. Recognizing real needs is a talent. Like Peter, Bob used to tell a story about his childhood. His earliest memory on growing up was his parents saying to him, 'Oh Bobby, stop asking so many questions.' Of course, he never has stopped and he can ask the most penetrating questions of anyone I know. A questioning mind can lead to a fountain of opportunities."

Mike was impatient. He was no closer to the magic formula than he had been two days before. Of course he was wrong. We now had two cornerstones to build on: constantly looking for opportunities and determination to find a way to capitalize on them. I could see that this was indeed a way of thinking that most people shunned, choosing to ignore possibilities or writing them off as unattainable.

That was it for today. The golf game had shortened the discussion. Afterwards at the Deli-Caf, Mike complained. "That golf idea was a waste of time. I hope Sam really opens up soon. I think he's holding back."

Terry was smiling. "Not really, Mike. I can't tell you how many times I think about that little golf exercise when I'm facing a problem. It reminds me that I can face new challenges, learn new things, and solve all my problems if I set my mind to it. The thought that I can't do something rarely come up anymore. I guess focusing on *how*, not *if* is really just a form of positive thinking — kind of critical, if you want to succeed."

Mike didn't sit around to discuss it. After wolfing down the usual coffee and Danish, he left the three of us to dissect the lesson of the day. Grace and I agreed on one thing: Sam was encouraging us to expand our thought process, and we both liked it.

We ended up leaving early that night. I had to barbecue at a shoreline party and Grace had tickets for a play at the local summer stock theater. Terry was the most reluctant to leave. He was clearly enjoying reliving his own sessions with Sam. Maybe he didn't have anywhere to go? Just three days in but worthwhile developments seemed to be happening. Grace confided in us that she had found a storefront at home that had enough space for her to start her first Blend a Good Yarn. She had a week to decide about leasing it. Her revelation kind of shocked me. I loved what Sam was doing and my stress level was way down, but I wasn't that close to taking any action. I had to admire Grace; she looked happy about the store, not worried at all. There wasn't any time to discuss it that night, but I knew we would talk about it often that week.

CHAPTER SEVEN

The Travelling Man

A long line of kids, anxious to water ski that morning, made me late, so I was the last to arrive the next day. As I entered the classroom the others were deep in discussion about Latin America. For once Sam was talking about his own experiences rather than describing one of his various "friends." As I sat down, he explained that he was describing his first trip to Argentina and Brazil that he had made in 1984.

"We tend to think of South America as the third world, but on that trip I visited three of the twenty largest cities on earth: Buenos Aires, Sao Paolo, and Rio de Janeiro. Besides falling in love with hearts of palm salad, the trip was quite an eye opener. The climate was fantastic, the beaches in Brazil went on forever, the people were warm and friendly, and the resources seemed unlimited. Yet we classified both countries as underdeveloped. Why do you think we did?"

Lowering my eyes, I tried to remember my high school geography. I really didn't know much about South America beyond the names of most of the countries. I never could get those three small ones at the top right. We didn't trade with any of them very much, so who really cared? Mike had no such hesitation. He immediately announced his gut feeling. Mike was far more preoccupied with feelings than facts.

"They're hot headed nut cases down there. Who even wants to trade with them? Look at Castro or Hugo Chavez. They don't have business leaders. Who ever heard of an entrepreneur from Argentina?"

Watching Sam roll his eyes at Mike's comments was becoming an everyday occurrence.

Before Sam could slam him, Grace jumped in with her own idea.

"First of all, Cuba isn't part of South America. However, I'm pretty sure that political instability was a major reason we considered them third world countries. If I remember correctly there were a lot of military juntas running those countries around the time you were there."

Sam smiled, pleased that one of us had some knowledge outside our own country.

"That's right, Grace. Mike couldn't be more wrong. There were tons of entrepreneurs in both countries. The problem was that none of them trusted their government. Every trade I made in those countries was paid for by transferring funds into either a Swiss or Dutch bank account. My business friends only transferred the bare minimum back home, just what was needed to keep their local factories operating. Their profits were not re-invested the way they should have been. As a result, the countries lacked infra-structure. Why, I even had the dubious pleasure of crossing an alligator-infested river outside of Sao Paulo in a car driven on to a ferry that was an oversized raft pulled across the river on a rope drawn by a donkey. We stayed in the car. It was an experience, but not one conducive to economic development. The investment in infrastructure was dismal, at least outside the core cities."

Grace was absorbed in the discussion. "If they kept their profits in Europe and paid no taxes, how did they treat their employees?"

Sam was relishing the conversation.

"That reveals a lot, Grace. The office staff, those who spoke English and were involved in dealing with exports, were paid in stable American dollars and were well paid with no worries about the high inflation that plagued both countries. At the time a good secretary who spoke English could make thirty-five thousand dollars a year. Those who worked in the factories or at more menial jobs fared poorly. A factory worker might make two hundred and fifty dollars a month, but they were paid in local currency, which was deflating daily against the U.S. dollar. Their wages always lagged behind the rising costs of living. Values changed by the hour and there was an active black market in currency transactions with visiting foreigners. On that first trip there were old peso notes and new peso notes in circulation that looked similar. They differed by a factor of a thousand, so you had to be careful, but I did bring one million old peso notes for my kids. They were basically worthless.

"While I was there I visited the home of a good business friend who I had known for several years. I always considered him a fair and honest man in our dealings. We were preparing a traditional Argentine barbecue at his home as we talked over a glass of wine from the western province of Mendoza. In casual conversation he bragged that his house was worth about $2.5 million U.S., but when I asked him how much he paid his three maids, he admitted that he paid them just one dollar each per day."

Even Mike was shocked at that.

"My God. Who could live on so little?"

Sam nodded his head agreeing with Mike, possibly for the first time.

"It taught me to appreciate something that most of us take for granted. A stable society in which all its members are valued and provided opportunity is the key to the success of a country and its people. South American society mirrored the old privileged class system that so many of our ancestors ran away from in Europe. The business people that I met were innovative, but they were also several generations into their success. Fresh ideas were lacking. Our concept of entrepreneurship and the upward mobility that we value so highly didn't exist. The benefits of discovery all accrued to the rich and established but many of them were fat cats, anything but hungry for success. Political instability stifled entrepreneurial instinct. Fear and greed combined to severely limit the development of countries with huge potential.

"Free enterprise can be the catalyst for change and wealth creation, but don't forget that the fundamental emotion invoked for individuals in varying political and economic circumstances is inevitably greed, eventually leading to fear. Once you have wealth, the fear of losing it leads to a reluctance to share for most. Boom is greed and bust is fear. Boom leads to bubble. Bubble leads to bust. Bust leads to paralysis. Greed allowed my friend to rationalize living in an expensive house while paying his maids virtually nothing. Fear made him keep his profits in Europe. My apologies to Adam Smith and Ronald Reagan, but the free enterprise system does not provide all the answers regarding the wealth of nations. Unbridled free enterprise sustains a class system, ignoring a substantial resource in the form of the uneducated and the deprived, the very people who came to North America looking for opportunity. Without a balanced approach, entrepreneurship will inevitably be more limited and stifled in this type of system. Few people like you would get the chance to pursue your ideas unless you were born to privilege."

Of course he was right. We had the opportunity, we were just afraid to take it. Afraid we might go backwards, losing what we had. My interest increased as he continued.

"Things are finally beginning to change in Latin America. Investment in education is increasing. The business community is more inclined to re-invest. But old habits are deeply ingrained and not easily changed. Our developing global economy is a catalyst for change, both good and bad right around the world. In the east, average people are gaining opportunity as a middle class develops. In the west income levels between classes are no longer converging. The rich are leaving the middle class behind. Some of the middle class is falling into poverty. Greed is driving a wedge again, one that can do serious damage.

"That's enough of a history lesson. As Bob Dylan said, 'these times, they are a-changin'.' And now it's time for us to get back on topic. Do you have any questions about what you've learned so far?"

As always, Mike was eager to make his point.

"So far it seems pretty basic — if you have that entrepreneurial flair that some of us are born with, just look for opportunity and drive like mad to make it happen. Then the money will come."

More rolling of the eyes along with a mumbled, "One in three, there always has to be one in three."

Grace had her own comment as well as a question.

"I think I understand. Entrepreneurs can be trained, thank God for that. Then we have to look for ideas. We cannot be discouraged but must always strive to find a way. My biggest concern is the ideas. Every idea isn't a good one. Surely just pushing like mad won't work. In fact, clinging on to a bad idea must be frustrating and draining."

Grace was quickly becoming the star of the class. I think this issue really hit a nerve for her and for me. The crux of our indecision had been whether our ideas were worth the effort. Sam knew it. I'm sure it was the most common problem that brought people to see him.

"Thanks, Grace. The biggest reason for failure among small businesses is pie-in-the-sky daydreaming. Most of us confuse the perceptive nature of true genius with dreaming of far out possibilities. Future success has to be grounded in present realism. First about the merit of the idea itself, and secondly how it can be achieved. The opportunity or idea has to have real sustainable merit and the plan of attack has to be achievable. So add the adjective 'worthwhile' to the noun 'opportunity' and supplement the question 'how' with the phrase 'on what basis?'

"A lot of ideas are half baked and are driven to failure by people who believe that taking risks is all that's required to succeed and that easy money is the goal. In contrast many good ideas die on the kitchen table because of the fear of failing. It's a familiar duo — greed versus fear. Realism works in either scenario; it can limit greed and overcome fear. In today's economy fear is ruling the day. It always does when a bubble bursts. Greed has compromised our banking system. Not long ago, the banks were a true catalyst for small business. Bankers did their homework and provided the third party assessment that small businessmen needed. If a bank was willing to lend you money to pursue your idea, that was the blessing you needed. Bank approval overruled fear and bank rejection undercut greed. In today's era banks look for easier profits and rely on formula banking for their lending, not judgement. Good and bad loans alike are made based on rigid criteria. Judgement has been abandoned to play the percentages.

"Small entrepreneurs are always saddled with personal guarantees, which scare off many and punish those who do take ill-advised risks. Banks don't encourage the former or discourage the latter. Good loans are rejected while bad ones are made, all in the interest of averaging out. This statistical approach is handicapping entrepreneurship when we need it the most, becoming a significant limitation on small business. Yet who else will generate the jobs so essential for recovery? So be prepared for this when you meet your banker. Hold your plan up to the strictest test before you take the loan. But don't forget, all bank approval means is that your request falls within the parameters set by head office and that your banker has been able to obtain more security than he needs. The downside is all yours. Financially, it has become more difficult to start a business than it was forty years ago. One reason is because our banking system is letting small business down, leaving most entrepreneurs without alternatives, subject to vulture capitalism — being preyed upon by venture capitalists. More about that later."

Mike looked over at me, revealing his confusion, which wasn't that surprising considering our recent discussions over coffee. All this talk of planning and borrowing was complicated. All he wanted to do was make money hand over fist like his brother entrepreneurs. When I shrugged back at him, Mike just shook his head. I wasn't too worried about borrowing. I was pretty sure I could land a big contract from my current employer to expand their reach. In that sense I did have a plan grounded in reality.

Sam was in deep conversation with Grace who was facing some major decisions regarding her plan and costs. She was about to sign a long-term lease to get the space she felt that she needed. Sam was offering advice.

"Sorry, Grace, but you have to do a full assessment of the costs. Too many start-ups miss the boat on their costs. You have to take the emotion out of your decision and prove to your own satisfaction that your plan is feasible. This location is not your only option, so take the emotion out of your thought process. Be your own toughest critic, but don't confuse fear with practicality. Don't rely on the bank. Drive a hard bargain with the landlord and allow for the possibility that you might fail. Negotiate a clause in your lease that allows both parties to get out of the lease if three months' notice is provided. You have to build in some downside planning."

Then Sam noticed that Mike and I were paying attention again.

"Proper planning and assessment can save you a lot of grief. Hard work can't make up for bad judgement. What's one of the biggest myths about successful entrepreneurs?"

No one had the answer so Sam gave us a hint.

"Well, it involves two numbers seven and twenty-four."

I gave it a shot.

"To succeed you have to work 24/7 — is that it?

Sam smirked.

"And how realistic do you think that is? What do you think is one of the biggest mistakes small business owners make?

No one knew. Was it bad ideas? Not enough money? Not enough ability? Not enough experience? For a moment there was total silence. All three of us were sure we were doomed if we couldn't answer. Finally Sam's laugh broke the silence.

"Either not paying or underpaying themselves — how realistic is that? If you learn nothing else from me, make sure that you pay yourselves. Working without pay isn't worthwhile and it certainly isn't feasible for long. It's an unsustainable subsidy. Your business will never survive if you become an indentured labourer, nothing more than a servant to your dreams, artificially subsidizing a concept that would otherwise fail. When you find the answer to 'how' you will make your plan work. Make sure that the answer does not rely on any artificial premise, whether it be working 24/7 or working without pay. And for god's sake take some vacation every year. The idea that long hours and low pay are essential to start your business is a crock. You may well do it, but none of it will make up for a bad idea or a poor plan to achieve it."

Then Sam looked at his watch. It was ten past five. Another session was over. Mr. Everyday did not like overtime. His last comment was a slightly different version of his usual reminder. "Things are getting interesting. Make sure you're all here tomorrow. Commitment is one of the foundations of success."

That one might make my list.

CHAPTER EIGHT

Reality Check

When we arrived at the Deli-Caf both Mike and Grace were visibly shaken. Sam was taking no prisoners that day and had served up a strong dish of reality. Mike was well into his second Danish before I had taken a single bite of my Chelsea. Grace was almost in tears.

She spoke first. "Maybe I shouldn't sign the lease after all. Maybe I'm just not ready."

About then Terry arrived with tea for Grace, a hot apple cider for me, and the usual coffee for Mike — all no charge while we were attending Sam's sessions.

"Reality check day was a tough one for me too, Gracie. It took me a week to bounce back, but I did. Sam doesn't want to scare you or any of us. I've talked to him about this a fair amount. If you're in a small business you're usually on your own, so you have to be an effective devil's advocate. We can all rationalize but Sam believes that there's only one person who can fool you about your own business, and that's you! I don't know if he's told you, but for several years Sam was a consultant dealing strictly with independent business people. A few of them became very successful but most of them were underpaid and overworked and eventually unhappy. Sam wants you to take that lease but he also wants you to drive a hard bargain, protect your own backside, and make sure you don't get fleeced because you believe in your idea too much."

By that point Mike had finished the second Danish plus the coffee and was on his way. Sam's course was free and Mike was getting his money's worth. He just couldn't get past the premise that entrepreneurship was going to be his easy ticket. I wondered if he would make it through Sam's everyday directive to the end of next week.

Grace had a grin on her face.

"Sam sure had the bank pegged. I have to give personal guarantees. I haven't discussed this with my husband yet, but he has to co-sign the loan. Maybe I can get better terms on that lease. The location's good for me, but it's not in a mall with anchor stores that bring in all kinds of traffic. The landlord's going to have three empty stores out of ten. He doesn't think I know it but he needs tenants. I'm going to ask for a phase in period with a lower initial rent, maybe a two-year lease with a five-year option, and maybe Sam's right — I'll go for an early notice clause."

Terry was all smiles at this.

"Of course you can, Grace. After listening to Sam I did the same thing. This place had been empty for eighteen months. I had been ready to sign almost anything just to have the chance. After I listened to Sam, I ended up getting a two-year lease with two successive five-year renewal options and a first right of refusal if the owner wants to sell. It amazed me. Before that I was desperate just to get a lease. Sam made me realize something we can never forget. Things can go wrong. The best laid plans of mice and men and all that. Negotiate based on the downside scenario and cover the upside as best you can. For sure don't let your enthusiasm lead to commitments that make you vulnerable."

I decided to change the subject, asking Grace about the summer stock performance from the night before. The change was welcome. It had been a heavy day laced with practicality. The usual sense of optimism was tempered with a touch of concern, but at least fear had not won the day.

CHAPTER NINE

Opportunity Can Be an Unexpected Companion

Sam appeared a little uncertain when we arrived on day five. Initially he started into a new subject line, but then hesitated before continuing.

"Normally I don't go back over things, but last night I felt that you left here confused. Grace, you seemed particularly upset. How did I confuse you?"

I understood why Grace was hesitant. She'd come close to mastering her doubts last night but she was also conscious of her gender and didn't want to show weakness or indecision. We had talked about that the first day. There were still undercurrents of doubt among some men that women could make it in business. I didn't think that gender was a consideration for Sam, although it may be for Mike. I could see the wheels turning before she decided to speak up.

"It wasn't anything you said, Sam. I understand the need to be aware of opportunities and the critical importance of having the drive to capitalize on them. I get that both opportunity and methods have to stand up to tough scrutiny. Yesterday you hammered the issue of viability. It's just that I came here with my idea looking for confirmation and I'm confused. My doubts were fading, but given so many variables, how do I really know if my idea is viable?"

Sam gave her a reassuring smile.

"There are no guarantees. If your idea was a sure thing some-one else would already be doing it. That's the excitement and the key to the achievement. To create something out of your own mind, anything at all, and have others confirm the value, well that's simply the best. Risk may be an overrated aspect of being an entrepreneur, but it's still an essential part of the equation. All I can tell you is to do your homework, learn as much as you can, analyze the possibilities, and ultimately trust your instinct. Success will depend on your ability to adjust as you move forward. You can only start with a rudimentary plan — cover the basics, provide for flexibility. You'll have to adapt as you go. Full-scale business plans will come later. Things seldom develop exactly as we expect. My advice is to enjoy the ride. It won't be smooth, but if you want smooth stay on the sidelines. As for opportunity, sometimes it's staring us in the face and we just can't see it. Other times we see opportunity but miss the most obvious factors that can block it. Look for the ideas but don't assume anything."

This discussion was far too complex for Mike, who was no less fidgety but was becoming quieter every day. As for me, the conversation over the past twenty-four hours pretty much returned me to square one in terms of doubting my own idea. I hadn't expected such an emotional roller coaster ride from a simple cottage seminar. All I really wanted was a rubber stamp and an all clear to go ahead. That signal might come but the onus had shifted to me to test the waters first.

Sam could read the doubt on our faces, so he reverted to some personal anecdotes, attempting to reassure us.

"Right after I sold my first business I spent three years as an independent management consultant focused on helping small business owner-operators. One of the most interesting cases I handled concerned two young fellows who worked for a roofing company. Both were in their early thirties and both had a solid mix of experience and enthusiasm. They had worked together for over ten years, originally apprenticing at the same time for the principal commercial roofer in the area, who did most of the larger industrial and commercial buildings within a hundred miles. About a year before I met them they had left that company in tandem and gone over to a medium-sized roofer who wanted to diversify away from doing strictly residential by adding a division for commercial and industrial. Business had taken off. These two fellows were thriving on having more independence and were driving the growth. The company had doubled in size in just over one year.

"Their new employer was no fool. He wanted to tie them up so he offered them the opportunity to each acquire 20 percent of the business in three years' time based on a valuation to be determined at that time. They had to put out $100,000 each now as a down payment on the option. Both of them were excited about the prospect of becoming owners. A mutual friend sent them to me to assess the offer. What they hadn't considered was that they were going to grow the company, literally make it happen, even financing the growth with their down payment, while driving up the value of the purchase price only to pay more for their share, which was still a minority position — a bad bargain for sure. It didn't take many questions for me to point that out.

"Then I asked them the key question: 'How far will your $200,000 go towards starting your own business?' It was like unleashing two foxes in a henhouse. Light bulbs went off in their heads as the obvious possibility changed their mindset. That was indeed enough. They became tireless workers towards making that start-up work. The experience of the previous year starting a new division for their current employer was invaluable. But, even with their total years of experience, they hadn't recognized the real opportunity until an outsider pointed it out. Even the most seasoned managers can miss a golden opportunity staring them right in the face. It's one of the reasons sales people often take over companies. They are not inherently smarter, but they do have the outside contacts and the greatest access to opportunities. Inside managers are often isolated from the market. Some of the best ideas flounder without entree to a market.

"As for my roofers, I have rarely seen a start-up take off as well. But the lesson doesn't end there. Initially these guys really appeared to be equal. They had started in the first business together ten years before. Both developed under the same demanding teacher, pretty much in sync with each other. Each one estimated, sold, and managed their projects, both large and small. They were equally enthusiastic about the opportunity as they entered into their partnership.

"So what was the outcome? Probably not what you might expect. The company has become quite dominant in the industry both locally and far afield, but the partnership ended after three years. The surviving owner is one of the most adaptable, driven, hardworking entrepreneurs that I know. His former partner, who had almost an identical background and ability, did not agree with the pace. Frankly few people would. Perhaps the second partner could have stayed with the original deal that was offered, where he could maximize the impact of his ability within a stable framework, provided by an owner-operator other than himself. In the end he settled for having his own business on a smaller scale than his ambitious partner wanted. He too is successful, but on his terms. Regardless, the same opportunities can be very different for different individuals. Viability depends on more than analysis. Among other things, it depends on circumstances and personalities."

This story confused me even more. Grace also seemed uneasy, so I spoke up.

"Sam, I'm really confused. If people like those two, experienced in an industry, couldn't recognize their viability in that industry what chance is there that I can?"

Sam smiled back. "That's just it, Tim. Those two had no problem assessing the viability — they were missing the opportunity. Once they identified what could be done there was no stopping them. You do know your industry and you have already identified the opportunity. What are you waiting for? Grace you have done more homework than most people I meet. Of course you have to keep refining your facts over and over. Keep learning and keep adjusting and get valid outside opinions where you can from suppliers, customers, even competitors. You should definitely cultivate your competitors. Build the complete book on your business. Only you can do it. Downside plan, upside plan — one plan is never enough — adjust often and early. Mike, you'd better get some ideas moving because you are lagging behind the class here."

Mike shifted uncomfortably in his seat then jumped up and started pacing at the back of the room as Sam continued. We were used to his edginess, so none of us took notice.

"Let me tell you one more story that reinforces the argument for ongoing scrutiny and the importance of full and ongoing assessment and adjustment no matter the business and no matter your experience. This one concerns the storied career of my friend Tom. Ten years ago he was active in two completely unrelated businesses. Tom had partners in both but he was the senior partner in each one. The two companies were profitable and both had meaningful opportunities. One was in land development the other in manufacturing. Tom was totally immersed in the former, mired in dealing with the bureaucracy during the approval process, when the opportunity to acquire a competitor presented itself for the manufacturing company. He had the knowledge to assess the opportunity, but not the time. I knew him well since I had worked with him on a previous development project. Over lunch one day he outlined his quandary. He told me that he'd only given the details of the acquisition a quick once-over but at lunch he made one of the most damning statements I had heard during my consulting career, one you must never allow yourself to say or even think. He said: 'I'm going ahead. The acquisition's too good to turn down and worst case scenario, I can stand the loss.'

"Being able to stand a loss is a poor substitute for properly assessing the viability of any opportunity. It haunts me today that I allowed him to be so cavalier. The feeling of entrepreneurial infallibility is a real and dangerous phenomenon. No matter how many times you get it right, every opportunity needs a full and careful assessment. Gut instinct tempered by analysis is an asset; gut instinct left to its own means can be a disaster. Needless to say, the acquisition took down the manufacturing company. The real loss was not financial. The real loss for Tom was self-respect and self-worth stemming from the knowledge that he failed to give that opportunity his best effort and assessment. That failure drove Tom into a premature retirement, a victim of lost confidence. Maybe I could have prevented it if I'd only spoken up at that lunch."

The three of us were stunned by his empathy. The memory of his friend's failure and his complicity by not warning him clearly still bothered Sam. We considered Sam so sage and wise. None of us expected a story of failure, never mind a confession of bad judgement.

He didn't give us any opportunity to comment.

"That leads right into another fallacy regarding entrepreneurship that is nothing more than a rationalization for poor judgement and weak performance. Do any of you know the so-called one million dollar rule of real entrepreneurship?"

Mike snapped to attention and practically shouted out.

"You're not a real entrepreneur until you have made at least a million dollars and also lost at least a million dollars."

I had heard of it but hadn't given it much thought.

Sam gave Mike an angry look, mumbling something like "it's always the one in three that knows that rule."

Then he spoke out more clearly.

"If you get nothing else out of these sessions, you must learn that entrepreneurship has nothing to do with reckless abandon or incurring losses in the interest of making high-risk investments. Entrepreneurship is all about judgement and commitment. Only a fool takes satisfaction in incurring large losses. And remember that when you incur a tax loss, the word 'tax' is only an adjective. It is still a loss, still red ink, and it's not a good result. Mistakes can happen. Losses do occur. Circumstances will change and you must change with them, but never be satisfied with failure as the end game! Now, all of you get out of here for today and go see Terry."

Sam was angry, and for once he left first. Failure was not his favourite topic and the emotion of the day seemed to drain his energy.

CHAPTER TEN

The Tigers are Out of the Cage — Be Ready

There was no Terry at the Deli-Caf to see, so we didn't get a chance to vent on this fairly disturbing session until later. He had closed up early that Friday night, leaving all of us to go home with much to consider and no one to talk to about it. It seemed that even Sam could take his eye off the ball, only to pay the price. Sleep recharged my enthusiasm but didn't eliminate my stress. Despite the histrionics of the previous session, with day six on the horizon, I was gaining confidence again. Sam's statement that I knew my industry and that I had identified my opportunity had resonated. I was getting my head around a plan that should be viable with a downside that I could manage and was not too punitive. The daily coffee sessions with Terry and Grace were stimulating and just plain fun.

Sam was drawing me out of my shell and it felt good! Ideas were flowing. Dreams were looking more and more possible. Positive attitudes were contagious. Now I understood the need for a valid initial plan — an action plan to match my ideas and my determination and a framework for evaluating progress. Regardless, I woke up that morning in a cold sweat wrapped in the realization that there was much more to be done and not much time to do it. Even a morning of mindlessly driving the boat for skiing and tubing didn't change my mood regarding the time pressure, so I arrived at the school in a bit of a black humour. I felt positive but doubts about timing had crept back into the equation.

Before Sam could start, I raised my concern.

"Sam, yesterday was pretty dramatic. You drove home a powerful message about proper assessment. I get the need but how are you going to help me convert my great idea into a feasible plan in one more week?"

Sam just smiled back, shaking his head in the process.

"First of all Tim, *we* are not going to develop the plan, *you* are. And secondly, let's just work through my sessions and see how you feel about this by the end of next week. Is that okay? Whatever plan you come up with, it will change radically. Just don't miss the obvious pitfalls before you start. Build in flexibility and be ready to adapt."

What was I going to say? Grace seemed to have her plan and Mike probably never would have one. Was Grace going to be the entrepreneur from this class while Mike flopped around looking for the quick and easy way, leaving me in limbo in the land of maybe? No way when this was over I was not moving into the realm of "what could have been." I guess the determination that Sam was preaching had caught a foothold in my thinking. At that precise moment I knew there would be a plan and I would be the architect. I had just reached my decision — I was going ahead.

In the meantime, Sam moved on to other things.

"We've been talking a lot about opportunity. Do you think that one good idea can sustain a business?"

As usual Mike jumped in first, certain of his answer.

"Absolutely! That's my goal; find that one big idea that's going to set me up for life. That's entrepreneurship and that's exactly what I'm going to do!"

I knew better. Part of what I had been wrestling with was sustainability. How would I be able to replicate the initial success about which I was confident? I needed more than one client. I had already watched Terry and Grace adding to the foundation of their initial ideas. I thought I knew the answer so I spoke up.

"Most businesses will die on the vine in this fast-moving global economy without ongoing creativity and innovation."

Grace jumped in to support me.

"Tim's right. Being an entrepreneur is not about the quick hit. It's about follow through and building up. It's about even more ideas and even better ways to accomplish them. I can feel that when we talk every night after we leave here. There's a mindset and an ongoing process involved. A philosophy is evolving dependent on accomplishment."

Sam was clearly pleased, and not just with Grace since he gave me a knowing nod and then continued.

"Of course you're both right. Ongoing innovation is the life's blood of entrepreneurship. North America and the United Sates, in particular, has been the spark plug of innovation for the last century, as well as a magnet for talent. Before that it was Britain, starting with the Industrial Revolution. Over the last fifty years America has spent almost 40 percent of the total spent around the world on research and development. In contrast the Chinese economy as it exists today relies on copying not creating. It shouldn't surprise any of us since both the United States and Canada are nations of immigrants. But far more than that, by definition our ancestors as well as our newest immigrants have been risk takers coming to a strange land for opportunity determined to succeed no matter what it took. Is it any wonder that entrepreneurship runs so deep in our veins? Opportunity, determination, and risk, sound familiar? We thrive on free enterprise and entrepreneurship is the engine of the free enterprise system."

We seemed to have lost Mike again, but Grace and I were intrigued. She spoke first.

"So you don't think the Chinese are a huge threat to our future? What about India?"

Sam was enjoying this exchange. You could literally see him switch into lecture mode.

"Oh, I would never write off the Chinese that easily. Like the Japanese and the Koreans have already done, they'll become more innovative, but it will take time in their culture. As their domestic market matures they'll continue to focus on mass production of concepts developed by others. It's their nature. India is a different story. I have travelled there many times and done business there for over twenty years. China is structured with large factories, basically joint ventures with the government and foreign interests. India is much more a country of owner-operated companies, innovative by nature. The best engineers in the world graduate in India. In that sense India could be a greater threat to us. But returning to my key point, both of these markets bring major threats and great opportunity to the table. Believe me, every threat is an opportunity and it is innovation that will open these huge and growing consumer markets for us, creating new markets not yet available. Globalization will reward specialization and assure efficiency through competition. Be ready!

"There will always be voids in the market. Often these opportunities will be too narrow for large companies, at least initially. The global economy thrives on change, which rewards, even dictates, flexibility. Those who are fastest through these windows of opportunity will thrive. Large corporations may be the end result but the chances for successful start-ups will multiply. Don't be afraid to look for connections around the world. We are about to move off the top of the pyramid. As for India and China, I've been fortunate, having done a fair amount of business in both countries. We do need to fear a tipping point with both. Their dependence on us as consumers will collapse to our detriment if we don't cultivate their markets.

"I've never really connected with the Chinese. My company could never offer them enough volume. In all my visits there,

I didn't make a true friend in business. No feelings of loyalty or continuity developed. Business was all about today, always about what exists now, never about what could be. I always felt this was a contradiction because the Chinese are known to plan over several generations. This paradox suggests that their dealings with the west are a means to an end and not their long term goal. If so, we need to be ready for a change in direction. They are very different people. The Chinese are so serious, consumed for the moment with immediate high volume.

"When it's convenient, they treat the west as an unending growth market, but their leaders see the enormous growth potential in their domestic market. As the United States borrows from them in huge volumes, they are investing a significant portion of their foreign reserves to buy up resources around the world. For now, the factory managers rely on the long production runs only the U.S. has been able to offer. The Chinese still do need the west, at least for now, but they have never fully accepted us. Expect the tipping point to come as their domestic economy expands. I'm afraid they will abandon us when it suits them and we will pay a heavy price for crawling into bed with them at the expense of many other relationships. We've given them much of our manufacturing know-how and lost it here at the same time. A day will come when they don't need us. Be ready!

"In contrast, the Indians embrace us, while too often we choose to rebuff them. But why do we? The Indians are much warmer, are easier to get to know, have a great sense of humour, many of them own their own businesses, and they are not co-authored by their government to the same degree. They have pride of ownership and love their businesses as much as we do. I have made many friends in my dealings with Indian companies. The Chinese are rigid, the Indians more flexible. My Indian friends simply don't understand why the west deals so extensively with China, the world's largest communist country, while choosing to ignore India, the world's largest democracy. I could never give them a credible answer. It's illogical on most levels but there is one undeniable reason — volume. The Chinese worship volume and they can deliver in huge numbers. No doubt there are other reasons."

Sam was engaged in story telling this morning. The three of us enjoyed his stories of travel and conducting business around the world more than his drier sessions on entrepreneurial behaviour and decision making. We valued both, but there was a lot of entertainment value in the accounts of his travels. In a way he was the last of a breed. The world was shrinking much faster, moving toward homogeneity, energizing but less interesting. His generation had the advantage of access to the world when it was still rather raw and unknowing, ignorance in the true sense. A world made up of countries and cultures newly accessible but traditionally distinct. Trade was an age-old activity but the genuine opening up of the global economy had taken place throughout Sam's career over the past forty years. He had experienced so much change as it took place. Sam had lived the life of a modern pioneer, at least by my standards. His experiences such as crossing that river in Brazil on a ferry pulled by a donkey, or shopping in a Bangkok mall standing out as the only white person at six feet tall in a sea of people five foot two or less, or visiting a small factory in Paraguay miles outside of Asuncion staffed by the Guarani would not be available to us, quickly disappearing, as the world continued to integrate. In themselves they were insignificant vignettes, but they were reminders of how fast things were changing. He was quite spellbinding that day as he continued his story.

"My first trip to India was in 1998. Perhaps it was my last personal frontier. At least it felt like that as I arrived on my own at three o'clock in the morning to an almost empty airport, exhausted after twenty plus hours of travelling. That feeling of serenity in a quiet airport didn't last long. Things remained tranquil until I collected my luggage and walked through the exit, outside into a throng of chaotic people waiting for arrivals, waving signs, and yelling on both sides of barriers that extended close to a hundred yards, or so it seemed. It was like walking the gauntlet. It seemed that those waiting for arrivals were not allowed inside. I had never met the gentleman who was picking me up. I knew his brother who lived in New York. The further I progressed the more I realized that I had no idea what I would do if he didn't show up. Of course he was on the sideline as I took my last few steps, patiently waiting holding a sign with my name. What a relief!

"The trip to the hotel was eerie. This happened barely ten years ago but things have changed quite dramatically since. At the time, street lighting there was dull with almost a muted orangey hue about it and there was no one in the streets so late. Driving along the deserted streets in the subdued lighting was unnerving, quite a contrast from the chaos at the airport. I had hardly settled into my room when there was a brownout leaving me in a dark room. Fortunately my wife had insisted that I take a flashlight. She also made me take a horde of granola bars and other snacks to avoid eating the local food and a bottle of Imodium in case I couldn't. The bars were all gone in three days and the Imodium was well used thereafter. The next morning I was picked up for my first appointment. There is only one way to describe the scene along the way: bedlam — throngs of people, five rows of cars in a two lane road, cows wandering in the street, incessant honking of horns, dust in the air, buses loaded to the hilt and myriad scooters, most carrying at least two riders, the passenger often being a lady wearing a sari, sitting side-saddle behind her husband or boyfriend.

"The images were fascinating but overwhelming. The rate of change since 1998 and the rapid emergence of a middle class since that time are beyond belief. What took the west over a hundred years to achieve is happening in closer to twenty years. Life is improving by leaps and bounds. Oh, there is much to do. There are two Indias, quite separate and distinct. Urban India is becoming well educated and able to encompass the global economy. Rural India faces a huge challenge in the form of education. It will take much longer to bring improvement to the poor and uneducated. Yet there is much demand for their unskilled labour to adapt to the requirements of the twenty-first century and fill the needs of the developing manufacturing and services sectors. India has a surplus of labour, which currently lacks the skills required. Almost every country has the same problem in different degrees. We certainly have it here. How do we become more skilled and what do we do with our unskilled workers?

We cannot be smug about this. Their need for education parallels the same one we face in North America, albeit in a much larger magnitude and with far greater cultural divisions. These are significant structural issues. Structural unemployment takes time to solve, if it can be solved. Here we need to educate people for high tech jobs for which we must compete. Even these won't come our way automatically. We are not competitive for unskilled jobs. In addition not everyone can be trained for these jobs. It may be politically incorrect to say so but we will always have unskilled workers. The educated class in India can already compete with us for the skilled jobs, making our challenge more difficult. The challenge to educate the rural population of India is to bring people out of an age old agrarian society and into the job market first in factories and who knows from there as they become educated. This is a tremendous potential resource for the country that will certainly be unleashed through education.

"Entrepreneurs in North America, just like you, focused on small business with a local niche must understand the framework of this global economy. Big business easily straddles borders and continents. North America is not an economic island. Integration into the global family is an important challenge for our emerging entrepreneurs. Finding likeminded associations around the world is critical for small business."

Sam hesitated for a moment, a big smile on his face, than he chuckled out loud.

"I was just thinking of an entrepreneur in India that picked the wrong project. This is a good lesson for you — sometimes success can literally bite you back. If you ever get a chance you can visit his rather sizable miscalculation in south India. His chosen market niche was a crocodile farm, a reptile zoo, to which he brought every type of crocodile and alligator you can imagine, all in well-constructed pens, safe for viewing. The climate was perfect, almost too perfect. He charged a decent admission price and initially he did very well. The only problem was that this particular inventory multiplies and literally eats up all the profits. Worse, the inventory is made up of endangered species that cannot be released because they are a threat to man and cannot be killed. Our entrepreneur tried to release some and was fined when his former tenants attacked some fishermen. Eventually he did receive subsidies from the government but the business was not exactly viable on its own merit."

We shared a good laugh at the expense of our Indian colleague. I'm sure it was a painful lesson for him and one not to be forgotten by us. Sam extended the meaning of the lesson for our benefit.

"Our Indian friend grew his business too much. Remember, when you're growing yours that overheads are exactly like crocodiles; they can eat up all the profits."

It worked. I still think of the crocodile farm every time I consider expanding. Sam returned to his script.

"Not so long ago, less than fifty years, one could carry on all one's business within a radius of five hundred miles. For most, all the suppliers and customers that a small business required were within that area or even less. You knew your competitors. They operated within that same area. Now we have to be much better informed and far less introverted. Actions taken thousands of miles away can make us impotent or create new opportunities. Challenges come from all directions. Together India and China constitute a third of the world's population and they are very different. The Indians are very determined to outperform China but are also becoming interested in the Chinese market for their products. Despite representing one third of the world's population, these emerging powerhouses are early in their evolution as consumers and represent far less than one third of consumption. That too will change. Be ready!

"However, for India, supply capabilities are often more fragmented than China, since more companies are smaller owner operated firms, generally less efficient than those of the Chinese. The current U.S./China economic alliance relies heavily on a match made in heaven, or perhaps hell. The U.S. buyer focuses on large volume to ensure low prices while the Chinese factories have been built and designed for high-volume production, making them able and willing to price down. They need each other. Cheap products made in volume to meet what has been almost limitless consumption. Neither country has other options as appealing yet. The result: a perverse debtor/creditor relationship that cannot be sustained indefinitely. As I mentioned, the Chinese are discreetly using their U.S. dollar reserves to buy and control assets around the world. You can see the threat. India offers more potential for our smaller independent entrepreneurial firms who will find willing trading partners there. You should keep this in mind. It's true for both goods and services."

Sam took the time to swish down some water. Time was flying by.

"I've gotten us more into macro-economic issues than I intended, but I hope the lesson isn't lost on you. In the same way that countries like ours have to make adjustments for changing markets and consumer needs, you have to do the same on a micro level within your own business. The market rewards innovation and punishes the slow footed. Your quest for opportunity has to be ongoing. Your rewards for finding new opportunities will be great but you will often have to go much further afield to find them. Your ability to execute new

ideas will determine the success and longevity of your entrepreneurship. Next week we will talk more about downside risk
and overstaying your welcome, but for today make sure you add
innovation to opportunity and determination."

At that point Mike emitted the familiar but unexpected sound
of a snore. He was sound asleep, no doubt dreaming about his
first big hit, oblivious to any threats and content to dream about
his future success. All the rest of us had the same uncontrollable
reaction, which was to laugh out loud, causing Mike to jump up
yelling "what was that?"

That was enough for Sam, who had spoken much more
than normal, determined to make us understand the reality and
requirements of the global economy. Today's session was over.
It had been intense but Mike had broken the spell.

"Mike you'd better head over to Terry's and grab a coffee. You
should have had one earlier. There's only fifteen minutes left so
this is a good spot to end. Tomorrow is Sunday so no session.
Monday we'll get back on topic and stop solving the problems of
the world. That's it for today."

What a pity. Today was invigorating. Entrepreneurship was
flourishing around the world even in the face of the Big Three:
Big Government, Big Business, and Big Labour. This was quite a
club that we hoped to join.

As we were leaving Grace went over to speak to Sam. I couldn't
help but overhear her.

"Sam, I've been working on my viability analysis for Blend
a Good Yarn. I have some personal doubts. We haven't talked
about this, but after nine years of broad experience and moving
up fairly well within a multi-national firm, I've been a stay-at-
home mom now for seven years. Sam, when I decided to go
back I couldn't get close to the same level, not anywhere, not
even with smaller independent companies. Seven years is an
eternity in terms of current experience. Do you think it's possible to move from being a housewife to a business owner in one

direct move? If no one else is willing to take a chance on me, should I be doing this?"

There was no hesitation on Sam's part.

"Of course you should, Grace, but this isn't a two minute conversation. No entrepreneur worth his salt is immune to self-doubt. Why, the first day you came here you told me that the fear of failing was more important to you than the money you might make. All of our fears are warnings that need to be put to rest. The fear of failure can either be a call to action or it can be a road-block that never allows you to get started. It's important that you harness this right now and use your natural fear to increase your determination rather than kill your initiative. Frankly I know more successful people motivated by the resolve not to fail than those bewitched by the joy of success. Why don't we talk about this on Monday? I have some suggestions. In the meantime, don't lose any sleep over this. We'll deal with it and I'm sure you'll feel better once we do."

It was easy to see that Grace was troubled. Sam might have reassured her more than he had instead of leaving her hanging for a couple of days. She was quiet on our walk over to the Deli-Caf. Since I didn't want her to know that I'd overheard her conversation with Sam, I just ignored her sombre mood, yammering away about one of Sam's last comments about emerging India.

CHAPTER ELEVEN

Mr. "One In Three"

Terry could usually lift our spirits. That Saturday was no exception. He was in rare form. It was Saturday night and we had a one day break in front of us. Since he had missed us the night before, he had more questions than usual. Mike had skipped the coffee and left for home, so it was just the three of us. Terry had cappuccinos ready and fresh biscotti, both new additions that he was trying. Terry introduced new items on Saturday when the weekenders were at the cottage so he could have the maximum impact. There was something new every week of the summer so it worked fairly well. His traffic always increased as people dropped in to see his newest idea.

Grace remained fairly subdued at first, letting me answer the questions until Terry started talking about Mike.

"Mike's a pretty important part of the class you know?"

Grace flinched at his comment while I laughed out loud before ridiculing the idea.

"What do you mean? He hardly makes any contribution. He just sits there and rattles of inane remarks and trivial comments about easy success. I don't think he's serious about any of this and I doubt he's getting much out of Sam's sessions. Mike has no idea what he wants to do. He's almost childlike and incredibly naïve."

Grace finally smiled, no doubt thinking about Mike falling asleep that afternoon in the midst of Sam's unusually long recitation. Terry was unrelenting.

"Sorry, Tim, but you're wrong. Mike represents the everyman who almost never acts on his dreams but still longs for personal success from owning his own business with no idea or real ability to go after it, no different than a would-be actor who has never acted, a would-be writer with no imagination, or a tone-deaf would-be singer. Mike is actually living his dream just a little by showing up for Sam's class. It may be the closest that he comes. He reminds me of some of the people who come in here every week to buy their Lotto tickets. For a few short hours every week they hold on tight to that ticket with the same chance of winning as anyone else and for a short time their dream of winning is alive. It's worth the price of the ticket to have the chance, to be in the running, even against all odds. While Mike is in your class, his dream is still alive. And when he walks out of that class next week he'll hold on to that feeling for quite a while. Sam won't start a session without someone like Mike. Sam needs the 'one in three' guy just as much as he needs the 'would-be' entrepreneurs like you."

That seemed doubtful to me.

"Are you kidding? Sam is always frustrated with Mike."

Grace was finally engaged, temporarily forgetting her own worries. "Maybe you're wrong, Tim. How many times have you heard Sam mutter something like 'there always has to be one.' At first I thought that he was being sarcastic, but more and more I think that he's reminding himself that Mike's presence is a necessary evil. Mike's totally predictable and so far he's been able to rattle off every cliché and misconception about entrepreneurs exactly when Sam needs it. In fact, that's practically the only time that Sam turns to Mike. It's like he's not a full part of the session, Mike is more of a teaching tool, which is kind of mean."

Terry shrugged his shoulders. He didn't seem to think there was anything mean about it.

"Is it mean? Much better than Mike paying out good money for someone to reinforce the idea that he is the entrepreneur he dreams to be, or worse, getting him to invest in some cockeyed scheme. He may not seem to be learning, but a lot of what Sam is saying will sink in."

That was more than enough about Mike and enough to lift Grace out of her funk. It turned out that Grace had backpacked around India back in 1990 so she had quite a few anecdotes of her own that reinforced some of Sam's stories. My favourite was about her state of mind during her first few days there, which she told Terry and me that night.

"I arrived in Madras, now called Chennai, with two other grad students in the middle of June. The temperature was well over forty degrees Celsius. We chose Madras for the cheap flights we could get out of London. The streets were just like Sam described, pure and utter chaos, dirty and dusty beyond belief. Some of the construction equipment we saw along the sides of the road looked like it was pre-Second World War. We didn't stay long in Madras, maybe two days. Then we were heading to Calcutta, now Kolkata, to try and see Mother Teresa and her orphanage. Everyone who had visited India that I knew told me that I would come to love this diverse country once I got used to her. I was forewarned about the culture shock and I thought that I was ready. I wasn't. I remember the three of us jammed into the back of one of the three-wheeled rickshaw taxis going to the airport. Sweat was dripping from our faces. The sounds in the streets were a cacophony of confusion. It was near dusk and the air was filled with dirt and grime. For that brief moment I felt that I was in hell."

The picture of a dishevelled Grace dripping from sweat in a dirty old taxi backpacking around India should not have been funny, but it was. Terry and I couldn't stop from laughing. The whole idea was so incongruent from the Grace we knew. Our reaction didn't faze her.

"Sam was right though. I soon came to love India, especially the people. I made quite a few friends there. We used to write regularly but now we send emails. Most of them are more computer literate than I am. All of the outsourcing we complain about happens for more reasons than low wages. Technology and education are creating a middle class where there was none. Their lives have changed dramatically. I hope to go back soon. And when I do I'm taking Sam's advice and looking for some business contacts."

We had no comeback. Neither of us had ever been out of North America. Once Grace found that out the sarcasm really flowed at our expense.

"How can a pair of morons like you two, who have never been anywhere, laugh so hard at my expense? Grow up! Maybe I'm the real entrepreneur here after all."

Given her mood earlier, that seemed the perfect note to end on. Anyway, I was late and so was Terry. As we left Grace smiled and thanked me.

"I know you heard me talking to Sam. I don't mind. He's right. I'll work this out, but thanks for being a friend and not rubbing it in."

Smiling back, I offered up the obvious. "No worries, you are the real entrepreneur in the class."

CHAPTER TWELVE

A Break and a Breakthrough

Sunday was a welcome break from thinking, at least for most of the day. Since I had no commitments, we made our annual family pilgrimage to the north end of the lake where we picnicked on beautiful Blueberry Island. Every year on the July holiday weekend our parents had taken my sister and me, along with two other families, and cruised up to the north end of the lake, loaded to the hilt with food and drink. The lake was stunning, so peaceful and natural, rocky granite shoreline, endless rising evergreens, and a whole series of unpopulated islands of which Blueberry was the shining star. In those days there were very few cottages at the north end, even on the mainland, and none on Blueberry Island. But there were two docks there, one perfect for docking our boat and a second one in deep water that was perfect for swimming.

It was idyllic, something we looked forward to each year. When I was ten I caught a five-pound bass there on my first cast. It was a beauty. On the way up we would stop in the middle of the lake and swim completely uninhibited. Further along, there were some cliffs overhanging the water. Every year we would swim into shore, climb those cliffs and jump from thirty feet landing in a deep pool of the most beautiful blue green water in a totally undisturbed area of the lake.

In 2009, the picnic was still a fun day, but things had changed. There was too much boat traffic to feel comfortable swimming out in the middle of the lake. There was a new monster cottage built on the cliffs, so no jumping. Worse, there were four boats tied up to each other at the boat dock and three more at the swimming dock on our island. So we enjoyed the picnic but it was laid out on the deck of our boat. Needless to say, some of the magic was missing. The trip did give me the chance to have a long uninterrupted talk with my wife Cheryl as we cruised back home. She had been supportive of my idea and my potential independence from the beginning. That afternoon the two of us were lounging in the cuddy cabin of my dad's old cruiser while our three boys were hanging out with my parents, taking turns driving the big ship.

"Do you know much about this Sam fellow, Timmy?"

I didn't really. No one questioned his credentials. There was no fee or any attempt to sell anything. All his stories seemed credible, certainly entertaining.

"I don't know much about him, Cher. The rumour is that he's pretty well off. But come to think about it, that came from Mike. Why do you ask?"

My lack of information about Sam didn't seem to bother her.

"Maybe it's because I like him!"

Now that was unexpected.

"How can you like him? You've never met him."

She rolled over toward me and gave me a kiss on the cheek.

"I like him because he's put a smile on your face, a spring in your step, and a plan in your head. Don't tell me you don't have one. I know you too well. So are we going ahead with Operation Seminar?"

She did know me too well and her support was a given. I was luckier than most. My spouse was not paranoid about losing our income. We'd already had a long talk about finances. Cheryl had a great job with the municipality and was now the third ranking bureaucrat in the transit authority. We wouldn't starve. She was a proven manager and my first sounding board for ideas. I had an in-house advisory board. Together we had plotted out the way I could approach my employer to secure their online training business as a foundation for what she loved to call "Operation Seminar." When Sam talked about third-party consultants, all I had to do was turn over in bed. It was time that I let her in on my latest feelings. It was hard to believe that it was only six days since I first met Sam. Quite a bit had changed in the week since we left home.

By the time we got back to the cottage we had agreed on the timing and the strategy. I would sit down with my immediate boss and the owner of the company right after vacation and lay out my plan and offer my new service. My heart was in my throat but I was thrilled, relieved, and afraid all in the same breath, but thanks to Sam, mainly excited.

That night I faced a more severe test. My parents were not risk takers. They knew little about my sessions with Sam and as far as I knew, nothing about Operation Seminar. Thank God I had my in house consultant with me to help me make that first sale. I'm not sure why parental approval is important. I suppose it's not for everyone. Maybe it's just so deeply ingrained from my childhood. I knew my parents didn't have the knowledge or background to assess the idea, never mind give their blessing. There was no doubt that the risk would scare them, after all their grandchildren were dependent on me. As it turned out there wasn't much time to prepare and I needn't have worried. They'd already done their share of that. Everyone knew what we were going to discuss. I had hardly asked them to sit down when my mother spoke first.

"I was talking to Terry this week. He seems very happy in his new career. I was asking him about Sam — he knows him very well. I just want you to know, Tim, that I trust Terry, and more importantly, I trust you. Of course I'm frightened for the two of you and the kids, but Cheryl has convinced me this week that you'll be all right financially. So I guess you should just do it."

This was going entirely too well and I hadn't said a word. The harder sell was still sitting on the couch, but I still didn't have to speak. My dad broke in right behind his wife.

"Tim, I've been watching you pretty closely since you got here. You arrived with the weight of the world on your shoulders. I've seen it disappear a little each day. Right now it seems to be almost completely gone, hopefully for good. Today you were our Tim again. Welcome back. Cheryl filled us in about Operation Seminar this week when you were in town. We think you should do it. Otherwise you'll regret it for the rest of your life. Anyway, we know you'll make it work. You were always meant to be your own man. We've known that for a long while, even if you didn't. Now, I got out of the market pretty early last fall, so I'm looking for an investment that I can believe in. I was thinking of investing in you. Can I help you out?

I was afraid to open my mouth. Cheryl had paved the way much better than I ever could. Things would only go downhill if I started to speak. I got up, kissed my mother, hugged my dad, gave my wife a longer kiss, and went searching for a bottle of wine and four glasses. I was literally speechless. How could I have come so far in a few short days? There was one more week with Sam and two more weeks at the cottage, then I would have to speak up and I would have to be at my best for that presentation. This one had been a little too easy with a far more receptive audience.

CHAPTER THIRTEEN

Surprise! Surprise!

Monday afternoon had arrived, back at the school, half way through our time with Sam with so much more to learn. As we arrived we noticed a petite dark-haired woman sitting at the back of the room. She nodded to us as we came in but otherwise didn't interact. As soon as we sat down Sam started. He seemed a little agitated.

"As you can see we have a guest, but with your indulgence I'll get to her later. We have to focus on the operational side of entrepreneurship this week, but not today. There's a theoretical side of entrepreneurship that I want to explore before we move on, which has many economic and political implications. Don't worry; I'm not turning academic on you. Theory and practice are reluctant soulmates but understanding the greater scheme of things can enhance results. This is a first. I feel strongly about my beliefs but I've never brought my theory into one of the groups before."

He hesitated, looked to the back of the room, seemingly for reassurance, and continued.

"My basic premise is that everyone has some degree of entre-preneurial skills or attributes varying from almost none for those who are stuck in a menial job with no ability or desire to move on, all the way up to Steve Jobs, who defined thinking 'outside the box' and is way on the other side of the equation. In between are the majority with varying skill levels. Can you accept this fundamental layout of the entrepreneurial landscape?"

All three of us exchanged glances, wondering where this would lead, before nodding.

Then Sam drew a free-hand bell curve on the blackboard labelling the vertical axis "% of the population" and the horizontal axis the "degree of entrepreneurial skill moving from low to high." His graph looked more or less like this:

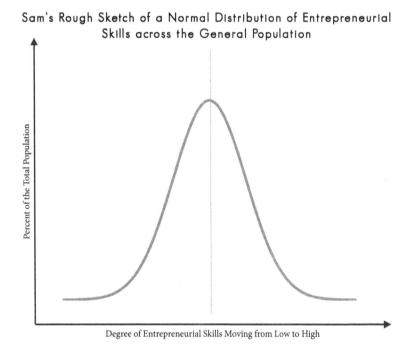

Sam's Rough Sketch of a Normal Distribution of Entrepreneurial Skills across the General Population

Percent of the Total Population

Degree of Entrepreneurial Skills Moving from Low to High

All of us have some degree of entrepreneurial skills.

Sam seemed eager for us to accept his argument and determined not to overcomplicate his explanation.

"On the left of this rough graph we can see that only a small percentage of humans completely lack the skills or traits that will help us succeed as entrepreneurs. On the right side a similar segment of the population has a very high level of the skills required, which, if allowed, could make them destined to become super successful. In between are the majority of us with varying skill levels, pretty much what you might expect for any skill set."

Sam was sweating profusely. He really wanted us to buy into this logic.

"I hope you have a basic understanding of a normal distribution used to represent the probability or likelihood of any event. In this case the curve provides a visual on how the entrepreneurial talent is spread out across the population. Have you seen a bell curve like this before?"

Once again all three of us nodded. This seemed to be going better than Sam had expected.

"My concept is not scientific, not yet, more of an abstract, but the curve is a meaningful representation of what I believe exists. Like any distribution as you move more toward the so-called mean or average position, the greater the numbers that have that particular skill level. The peak or top of our curve represents the average skill level with 50 percent on either side of the top point. You can speculate that Steve Jobs and Thomas Edison would be on the extreme right of the graph with the maximum skill level. Those few totally content to remain in humble positions and unable to change if they wished would be on the extreme left, and the rest of us somewhere in between. Now I'm moving fast, but this is critical; our graph only shows ability, not the application of the skills. That's the bigger challenge. How do we remove the obstacles for countless individuals around the world with talent and ability, specific to entrepreneurs? There are so many barriers that limit the use of entrepreneurial skills. That's the issue political leaders need to focus on. I know there are a few Edison types out there who are suppressed for all kinds of reasons. More important, there are large untapped numbers with abilities on the right side of this graph who are being stifled to the detriment of themselves and society. So if you found yourself in different circumstances and prospects as we know exist around the world, how would it impact you? For example, if you were born into a tribal society with a high level of entrepreneurial skills, would you be a businessman?"

Mike was fast off the mark, "No, I'd be the chief."

Sam gave Mike the most genuine smile he had shown him in a week.

"That's right, Mike, and if you grew up in the ghettos of a large U.S. city with a high level of these skills but little chance of an education or a good job, would you be a businessman?"

I took this one. "No, Sam. I'd be a gang member, maybe even a drug dealer."

Sam was smiling as he turned to Grace.

"And if you couldn't afford an education, married young, and were a housewife, would you be a business success?"

Grace accepted the challenge. "No, but if someone came into my house they might think I was Martha Stewart."

There was an infectious laugh from the lady at the back of the room at that.

Actually we all chuckled, especially Sam. I felt that I understood what he was getting at, so I spoke out.

"So you believe that everyone has at least some of what it takes to be an effective entrepreneur, but those who have the potential to be highly successful or even moderately successful might not get the opportunity. In fact, due to circumstances outside their control, many around the world, maybe even most, don't get that chance. I assume the corollary would also be true: those that get the opportunity don't always have what it takes. As a result many people with the 'right stuff' end up excelling in different ways within their own environment but fail to achieve their full potential. Is that it, Sam?"

Sam was nodding and so was Grace.

"More or less, that's it. But the tragedy is that entrepreneurship is the powerful economic engine that addresses critical economic issues that big government and big business ignore. Maybe it's the most powerful economic engine for positive change, especially in tough times like now. But we don't treat character traits as a resource. Economists talk in generalities about 'labour,' but in the case of entrepreneurship we need to make an exception. This quality needs to be recognized, encouraged, and developed! If you believe that entrepreneurship is a valuable resource for society, what factors do you think limit it, not just here but around the world? Just shout some out and I'll write them down."

In less than one minute we had the following list of limitations: education, finances, gender, race, training, jobs, location, culture, religion, health, technology, legislation, political instability, and communication. There were others, including the lack of role models and infrastructure in many parts of the world. These were social issues that society in general had to tackle.

Sam was shaking. "I feel so strongly about this. Entrepreneurs do not have all the answers, but they are the key to job creation. Small independent business will find niche markets and develop localized jobs that won't exist if big business increases its dominance. They are the key to solving structural employment issues. As the world becomes more integrated it's not possible to shift people to the countries that best suit their skills. Competitive advantages will determine which economic activities take place and where. Every country will need to find solutions for localized structural unemployment. One of the most difficult challenges of our growing global economy is to free the vital resource of entrepreneurship, including right here in North America. We are only scratching the surface of unleashing this natural resource, one that lies within us. The world has many more potential entrepreneurs, but they're being stifled by circumstances that can be changed. Even within the liberal, democratic countries, Individualism is underutilized and now it's being threatened by big government, big banks, and big business as well as a whole range of entry-level barriers.

"While these skills are utilized within the framework of big business and to a lesser degree within big government, they are not generally an integral part of the culture of these institutions. All of the 'Bigs' frown on unconventional behaviour and rely heavily on internal politics and structure in decision making and promotion. When you add in the Peter Principle, which recognizes that we all tend to get promoted to our level of incompetence and *stay there*, big is simply not better. We have to find better balance within the 'Bigs' as well as boosting the small independents. My graph may be simplistic but there's a spot for every one of us on that grid. The onus on entrepreneurs, those on the right side, is pivotal — do what comes naturally. Make things happen, in the process creating upside for everyone in society, not just for themselves. As for society, the onus is first to remove the barriers and unleash the catalyst that puts resources to work, but also to employ some of that same talent to make collective action efficient."

This concept did make for an exciting theory. How could you not want to become engaged in the process? Our society classifies the problems of inequality and lack of opportunity as social issues, but Sam was presenting them as economic limitations, not just for those directly affected, but for society as a whole. The idea was appealing: freeing up all the talent that was suppressed as I had felt. In my case the suppression was self-imposed, surrounded with opportunities that I failed to see or appreciate. How much worse must it be in other cultures to have the ability but no access to education or opportunity? Sam wasn't finished yet.

"So what do you know about laissez-faire economics and free enterprise?"

Mike was back right on cue.

"We need less government. The private sector can create more jobs and run things more efficiently than government. Get rid of tariff barriers, restrictions, and governance and let entrepreneurs do the job."

Mike was a great straight man for Sam.

"Thanks, Mike. That summarizes things fairly well. You probably think that I believe in free enterprise. And I do, but only as part of a balanced, mixed economy. You see, under a strict free enterprise system most of the entrepreneurial talent will remain suppressed and unutilized, just like the old days in South America. Individual entrepreneurs will be preoccupied fighting their own battles and finding their own success. They will rarely spend money or time to free talent for the greater good, at least not beyond their own needs. In the process of maximizing their own rewards, they do indirectly help society by creating jobs and introducing innovation. We simply need more of them. They are a great force, but not an altruistic one. Greed does not focus any individual on providing the same opportunity to others or promoting innovation and competition from more sources. Only government can attack the list of limitations we identified and unleash the real power of more entrepreneurs around the world.

"Self-interest is just that, and, as we've discussed at length, it manifests itself in greed and fear, producing false economies that need the leadership of government to moderate corrections. Society needs to free up every ounce of entrepreneurial talent we can find. Believe me, it's out there. We do have philanthropists who help and encourage others. But it's only through the collective action of government that we can deal with social issues like education, gender, finance, race, and the other cultural issues that limit initiative. Only government can unleash the total power of free enterprise. Ironic, isn't it? Entrepreneurs make things happen, but the world needs government to make this happen."

Sam was winded. This conversation had been a sprint. Grace had a comment.

"So, if I understand you correctly, we need government to free up more private resources to do the things that government itself either can't do or does poorly. Is that it?"

Sam nodded in agreement.

"More ironic is that free enterprise, left unchecked, through greed and self-interest will stifle the maximization of entrepreneurship, the very thing that their ideal society craves. But there's a further paradox in the need for government to adopt some of the positives of free enterprise by attracting these same skills and attributes, which naturally gravitate toward the private sector, into government to improve the efficiency and cost of governing."

Grace interrupted again.

"I think you're saying that the cost *to* society of *improving* society needs to be reduced, the key to which is bringing more entrepreneurial thinking into the management of government. So does the entire world need to free up entrepreneurial talent to utilize in both the private and public sectors?"

Now Sam was beaming; his star pupil of the week had tapped right into his theory.

"It goes well beyond that, Grace. Remember our beloved entrepreneurs act as catalysts. They are only part of the solution, but they are the means to get started, the key resource that makes things happen. If you look back at my graph on the board, we've allowed a culture to develop within government, a culture of bureaucracy staffed to a great degree by people on the left side of that graph that value stability, abhor risk, reluctantly accept innovation, and are suspicious of the private sector. We need to break the mould of that subculture and we need to structure reward systems that attract different skills into the public sector. For the private sector a budget is a target to reduce and the system defines success as 'coming in under budget.' In the public sector budgets are meant to be spent so they aren't cut in the future; coming in over budget warrants an increase in the next go around, not a black mark. Such an established philosophy does not manifest itself in efficiency and cost control.

"This dilemma is all about balance and integration. We need government to free the bonds so new and more entrepreneurs can develop while changing the culture within government to attract and welcome entrepreneurship into the fold. Don't misunderstand. The catalyst only gets things started. The more things that are underway the more benefits accrue to people on the left side of the curve and society as a whole. The goals are to create more economic opportunity for everyone *and* to ensure that government is cost effective and viable. We need a balanced economy between government and the private sector and we need balance within government between the attitudes of bureaucracy and free enterprise. We desperately need to rebalance. Can it ever happen?"

We all needed a break. Sam asked Mike and me to run across to the Deli-Caf for coffee.

CHAPTER FOURTEEN

The Better Half

Grace and I were blown away and a little wound up. Our discussion over coffee was heated and lively. Even Mike was excited and engaged in the debate. After a fifteen-minute coffee break, which he spent at the back at the room talking to the mystery woman, Sam was ready to resume.

"I can tell I've got your interest but as abruptly as it came up we've got to step back from theory and into the practicality of your world. You need some time to digest things, but remember every entrepreneur unleashed can be a step forward. But before we do get back to the program I have another first to accomplish. Grace, I hope you don't mind me telling this. On Saturday Grace asked me if she was making a mistake. She was questioning if she could make the jump from housewife to independent businesswoman. It's a very common concern. I'm happy to say that the recognition of entrepreneurship among woman outside the home is on the rise. We finally are getting more female CEOs, not enough mind you, but at least movement. More than that, women are really embracing small business and starting businesses at a surprising rate, despite funding limitations and a wealth of other issues.

"Freedom and flexibility provide strong motivation to exercise entrepreneurial skills but is the transition from housewife to businesswoman really a prohibitive leap? That issue leads me to my other first for the day. The lady at the back of the room is my wife, Robin. We've discussed this issue many times, but this is the first time I've asked her to speak to one of my groups."

With no further introduction, Robin moved forward from the back of the room, conscious of the scrutiny she was getting from Sam's latest protégés. He was six feet tall, blue eyes, fair hair, initially reserved, maybe a little intimidating. Robin was five foot two, dark hair, and brown eyes, vivacious and welcoming. We liked her immediately.

"Thanks, Sam. I can only say it's about time but let's get right to the point. Grace, be glad that you have the option. So many women around the world don't. Sam and I belong to a generation that straddled the traditional belief that women belonged at home and the onset of the women's liberation movement that belittled those wives who did. We wrestled with this same issue thirty years ago once our three kids were all in school. Would I go back to work? Would I start a little business of my own? Sam was already successful leading a business with two hundred and fifty employees. He always told me that running our home was operating a business and by doing it I was supporting him, allowing him to run what he called the 'outside' business. He called himself Mr. Outside and me Ms. Inside. I thought he was being patronizing. We argued about it more than once. Then one day he sat me down and we made lists of what we did in our respective jobs. Then he edited my list to put things in perspective. As I remember his list it went like this …"

She wrote on the board:

1. Set Strategy
2. Review Results
3. Solve Problems

"My initial list went like this:

1. Wake up kids.
2. Make lunch
3. Drive to school
4. Buy groceries
5. Make the beds
6. Vacuum the house
7. Repair leaky hose
8. Fix the toilet
9. Deal with kids problems
10. Make dinner
11. Make sure the dishes get done
12. Collapse

"Sam insisted my list was incomplete and he edited it. His version of the same items became:

1. Direct staff
2. Manage the cafeteria
3. Director of transportation
4. Purchasing agent
5. Controller
6. Manage and execute set up
7. Manage end of shift cleanup
8. Maintenance
9. Solve problems
10. Customer entertainment
11. Delegation to staff
12. No comment, but there are some other functions I'd personally like you to consider

"His conclusion: You are the generalist in our family wearing all the hats on the home front. We know whose job is harder. I've been there when my business was smaller. It's a revolving door to do it all. So this is about you doing what you choose because it's what you want.

"Those were his exact notes. I kept them. His point was right. The decision was about me — not the kids and certainly not women's lib. You're going to discuss operational issues this week, but having your own business means problem solving, filling every conceivable role, and long hours. Sound familiar? The graph that Sam drew earlier applies to a wide variety of situations, including households. The stronger your entrepreneurial skills, the more balls you can juggle and the better you can run your home and family life. It's a full-time, demanding job and if you can do it well, you can run another business. The same principles apply. Ms. Inside can certainly become Ms. Outside, or more likely both in a long work day. Things have changed since I made my decision. In fact, in today's economic and social environment, Ms. Outside would be my choice."

Her message was clear. I had no doubt that Grace ran a tight ship at home that would translate well into her business. Robin stopped there, but all of us wanted to ask her some questions about Sam.

Instead he wanted to add something.

"So much is made of the male entrepreneur. Our society still slants the odds of success in their direction and it's much worse elsewhere. But who applies their entrepreneurial talents more, a housewife or an accountant? Women who stay home and run a household effectively have to be determined, independent, and creative. Men working in a narrowly defined job don't have the same demands on those skills. We used to when we were hunters and farmers and literally had to find ways to make things happen, rather than being told how. You've heard the expression 'use it or lose it.' There's a new term kicking around called 'Mompreneur,' tied to women starting businesses. Groups of likeminded women are already building support networks for the large numbers of women dealing with the dichotomy of running both a business and a household. Maybe you actually have an advantage, Grace. We'll talk about that later. We're into overtime so we'd better wrap it up. Do you have any questions for Robin?"

Sam stepped aside to let Robin answer, moving outside to wait for her. When Sam disappeared, Robin noticed and wanted to go after him. We were gung-ho to learn more about the reserved Sam. She declined to come over to the Deli-Caf, but finally did agree to sit down with us briefly. Mr. Everyday was part of their tight knit team and we wanted to know more about him from the one who knew him best.

"Sorry guys, but I've only got a few minutes."

Grace was determined to make the most of it.

"All right. Tell us five things about Sam that will surprise us."

Robin was intrigued.

"Here's a list of things I think will surprise you:

1. When I met Sam he was seventeen. He was so shy he had a friend call me for our first date.
2. At university Sam never attended his tutorials for four years because the groups were too small and he couldn't hide in the corner unnoticed.
3. Sam was hired to be a professor at a small college and only turned that down to go into business to help my family when my father died. Business was never the plan.
4. First and foremost Sam is a problem solver. If there is a problem personal or business Sam wants to solve it, even when he can't.
5. Sam never proposed. Once in conversation he mentioned 'after we're married.'

"Surprised? Sam was an 'accidental' entrepreneur. He's a late-blooming natural who had no idea of his talent. He could easily have missed it all. So those are five things you never would have guessed about Sam, but here are five things you need to know about him if you're going to believe in him.

1. Sam was a gold medal winning student at university, captain of every team he played on, even the foreman of the jury he served on.
2. Sam has had successful businesses in manufacturing, consulting, retail, wholesaling, and land development.
3. As a consultant Sam shepherded several successful business start-ups.
4. This one sounds familiar. First and foremost Sam is a problem solver. If there is a problem personal or business Sam will solve it, if it can be solved.
5. Sam will always be there for advice and consultation if you ever need it.

"That's the best I can do, and if he finds out what I've told you, he won't be happy. He's a bit of an enigma, but you probably have figured that out. Good luck this week. I really have to go. Grace, make sure you go to the Deli-Caf today."

Great information, but we wanted more. Who would have thought that Sam had been so withdrawn? Or that someone who had a successful career as an entrepreneur had no intention of starting a business? That would have to wait. My list grew significantly that night.

CHAPTER FIFTEEN

Revelation

When we arrived at the Deli-Caf we were pumped. Robin had brought a refreshing change to the class and exposed a softer side of Sam. What a session. Sam's theory was a little heavy, but it was thought provoking. His concept tied government and free enterprise together in a way that none of us had considered. Was Sam a liberal or was he conservative? Could he be both? Or was he neither? If he was right, no pun intended, bureaucracy and the free market were interconnected in perverse ways. Perhaps interdependent without separation if they wished to maximize their distinct goals, bringing new meaning to the expression "politics makes strange bedfellows." It did make sense that a fully liberated free enterprise society could only be reached through the collective decisions made and implemented by government. There were too many barriers entrenched in various cultures that could only be changed through the will of society — a very liberal approach.

Was he also right that optimum and effective government could only be achieved on an affordable basis by introducing more of the skills and techniques inherent in an entrepreneurial environment? If so, this made an interesting pair of economic oxymorons: "efficient government" and "subsidized free enterprise." Each one depended on the other to reach their potential — what a delight. If so, government action was the answer to releasing entrepreneurship held hostage by a wide range of factors, and attracting additional, more independent thinkers into the existing bureaucracy was the solution to making government viable. In the simplest terms, these traditional adversaries needed each other.

On a more personal level, Robin was delightful. She brought a new dimension to Sam and a greater understanding of his anonymity. The last thing she said was intended to put things into perspective.

"Remember, entrepreneurship is a powerful, underutilized resource, but it isn't the cure for cancer. I know it actually could be, but whatever. Maintain balance in your lives. Sam does. I make sure of it."

Naturally, she was right. We weren't about to change the world, but maybe we understood it a little better. Maybe we understood ourselves significantly more. Regardless, we all felt a change and a connection, well beyond our own plans. Of course, Mike still didn't have any.

Grace was in a much better frame of mind when Terry came over to greet us. We were sure we had some new information for him but I was surprised at his reaction to our account of the day as we described meeting Robin and listening to Sam's theory. He seemed a little edgy and was almost dismissive.

"Actually, I've met Robin quite a few times. She's a dynamo and a great partner for Sam. As for the theory, at first it seems like a revelation but I'm not sure how it really comes into play. There are so many barriers to unencumbered entrepreneurship. And how practical is it to stream different skills into government agencies? Bureaucracy is so deeply entrenched."

We were all perplexed at his response. He was always supportive of Sam's ideas. Was he playing devil's advocate, or was he just distracted? I decided to call him out.

"How is it that you know so much? Sam said he's never talked about his theory in class and supposedly this was the first time Robin's talked to one of his groups."

Terry shrugged. "Well that's all true."

He was acting a little odd. I had known him the longest and he was hiding something.

"All right, Terry, come clean. How do you know so much?"

Just as I spoke, an attractive blond woman walked in the front door, unusual at this time of night because Terry almost always closed before this. He didn't miss a beat.

"It's her fault."

What was he talking about? None of us had ever seen her.

"Really? Who is she?"

Just then the blond came over towards us.

"You must be Grace. Robin asked me to stop by and speak to you. I'm Jennifer and I'm married to the coffee magnate here."

Whoa. All of us were caught off guard by that. I spoke first.

"I thought you were separated and your wife lived in the city?"

Terry looked a little sheepish.

"Well, technically we have been separated, but Jennifer's been here the whole time. Robin probably told you that Sam is a problem solver, and he's been part of our solution. Maybe you can fill in the blanks, Jen."

Jennifer didn't hesitate.

"I feel like I know you all, so why not. Two years ago I was totally unhappy. Terry had a good job selling real estate in the city. You've probably guessed that selling is his strength. But his job meant lots of weekend and evening work. I'd been at home for eight years with the kids, just like you, Grace. I had the housewife routine down, believe me I was organized, but I wanted more and his hours were crazy leaving me on my own too much. I was desperate for a change and I was ready to leave Terry if I had to do it. That's when Sam got involved. He knew us both well enough. Terry had told him about this area. He helped the two of us map out the Deli-Caf, and that probably saved me and us."

There were still a lot of unanswered questions.

"But you're never here. Terry runs the Deli-Caf. How has it helped you?"

Terry smirked at me.

"Timmy, you of all people should understand that and you should have suspected something. Remember when we ran the trash business? I got the customers and you did the slugging, right? I was always a starter, not a finisher. You must remember. Well some things haven't changed.

"Who do you think gets up at two o'clock in the morning to do all the baking? Who orders all the supplies during the day when I'm in here glad-handing? Who do you think finds the new products we bring in every weekend? Have you ever seen me on the computer? Who do you think researches new websites and writes our blog? You're looking at the real entrepreneur in this company. Jen is amazing." At that point she was also was blushing.

"There's no doubt — this business saved me and saved our marriage. When we first moved here we stayed separated. I rented a cottage ten miles down the road and kept under the radar. I was sceptical that this crazy idea would work out. The life is exhausting but invigorating. We have the nights together and there's so much to talk about, much more to share than before, and there's lots of time for rest in the winter. We've been apart but we've never been so together. I moved back in with Terry last weekend. Our kids are ecstatic and so are our parents. By the way, did I mention that Sam and Robin *are* my parents?"

There was a stunned silence. Then Mike spoke up. I'd almost forgotten he was there.

"I thought so. You look like Sam." Actually, she did.

"Sam's been worried about you, Grace. You know he's on a crusade to promote entrepreneurs. It's on a small scale, but he's been making progress. I think my problems have changed his mind in several ways. Now every class has to have one woman in it. He was never a chauvinist, but deep down I'm sure he doubted that women had the right stuff. They were quietly shifted to the left side of the curve, as he likes to put it. That's changed! Woman entrepreneurs face different barriers, especially the interruption to their careers to have a family. With the speed of change and globalization that disruption has become more limiting, pushing many women toward safe careers in government and other areas where it's easier to resume. The only problem is that in big government and big business we're almost interchangeable, like plug in parts, modular and uniform. Roles are defined to facilitate the modularity. You've experienced the frustration first hand. It's hard to get back into play. Younger, more current versions are preferred.

"After my experience and frustration, Sam has become more aware that women often push their entrepreneurial skills where men hesitate, because they have to find alternative work. He calls it entrepreneurship of necessity as opposed to entrepreneurship of opportunity. There are exceptions, now more than ever. Women do get executive positions, but too often we don't get the opportunity or can't wait for it. Right now that still means too many restaurants like ours or craft stores like yours where the failure rate is high, but Sam sees that changing. There has to be better options than providing cleaning services for other working women. Of course there are and we women do have our successes. He and I have talked about you, Grace. We talk about every woman in his sessions. He thinks your yarn store is just the beginning for you. He wants both of us to become role models. That's why he got my mom and I involved today. Maybe its guilt or maybe it's just his preoccupation with solving problems, but he's determined to encourage more female entrepreneurs, especially, to seek out more and better opportunities."

Soon these two instant friends were in deep conversation, sharing stories of frustration and ambition alike, while Terry quietly cleaned up. It seemed like a good time for Mike and me to leave. When we did it seemed to go unnoticed.

CHAPTER SIXTEEN

A Race to the Finish

Five days left.

Sam was in a hurry to get started that afternoon. That was the pattern for the rest of the week.

"You need to know that we're behind schedule. Yesterday was a diversion, an important one, but not part of the program. Maybe it should be, but that's a different question. So today we're back to basics. What have you learned about entrepreneurs so far? Grace, would you like to summarize for us?"

Grace was ready, no doubts on the horizon. Yesterday had been for her benefit and she knew it.

"We've learned that we should have tons of ideas, the importance of separating real opportunities from ideas, the need to assess the viability of the opportunities, and most of all the determination to make things happen and capitalize on the worthwhile opportunities."

Sam nodded. "Not a bad summary, but where does this leave you in terms of accomplishing anything?"

I had been thinking about that on the way into town that morning, so I spoke up.

"We're still in the planning period. We need to move into implementation. As Terry would say we're in his phase: the start-up mode. Now we have to become the operators and move into my phase and Jennifer's: the finishing stage."

Apparently this is what Sam wanted to hear, because off he went.

"Get ready. You've heard them used a lot over the past week but you're going to get sick of the words 'entrepreneur' and 'entrepreneurship' this week. Sorry, there's just not a good alternative — lots of synonyms but no good equivalent. Even the synonyms are types of entrepreneurs, not definitive enough. Whenever entrepreneurs are discussed you always hear about innovation, foresight, and risk taking. You rarely hear about process. For the next few days we're going to talk about more basic entrepreneurial skills that make things happen. Maybe 'movers' and 'shakers' are the best alternative terms for our heroes because that's the very crux of entrepreneurship and the essence of why it is such a powerful resource.

"Entrepreneurs are agents of change; they make things happen. They are the catalyst that makes the economy function, the driving force that channels other resources into productive activity. They employ labour and pay wages. They borrow capital and pay interest. They buy raw materials and convert them into products. They are the origin and foundation for most large corporations, although they are often long gone by the time these companies mature. They are the agents that find the practical applications for others' innovations. They create markets that didn't exist and products others couldn't imagine. They are conduits of information around the world and open up trade to find opportunity. They also come in all shapes, sizes, genders, and races and bring quite a variety of skills.

"So let me tell you a cute story about determination and making things happen. A good friend of mine was in her first year of teaching. She was a physical education major, so her main subjects were physical education and health. She was and is a very pretty woman. Whoever established the schedule had a sense of humour because they gave this greenhorn teacher a class teaching health to a co-ed class of sixteen year olds. Awkward for her, but the boys quite enjoyed it. One day a future entrepreneur in her class presented a challenge: 'I bet that I can kiss you without touching you.' There was quite a buzz around the room at this. Well, my friend, novice that she was, took the bait. 'That's not possible.' After some discussion they agreed to bet five dollars. Where upon the student came forward, gave her quite a kiss, full on the lips, handed her the five dollars, and walked out of the room to the cheers of all his friends. Now that's a great example of determination, innovation, seizing the opportunity, and making things happen. Ten years later he came back to the school and dropped in to see my friend, took her for a ride in his Mercedes, and then on a tour of his newly opened factory producing auto parts. His success didn't surprise her. The surprise had come ten years before.

"All these stories and examples of entrepreneurial glory are glamorous, but your reality starts in the trenches. For the next five days we're going to review a check list of practices and methods that I feel are critical for you to become successful entrepreneurs. Some of these things will be second nature for you, others more difficult, a few impractical. What you can't do well should be addressed in your team building, but that's a topic for later this week."

This segment was perfect for me, exactly what I was hoping for. With Cheryl's support I had made the decision to move ahead. I knew that I had the right opportunity. It was fully vented with Cheryl, my friends, my parents, and supported by hours of self-analysis. I was confident that my plan was viable, equally sure that my risk was moderate, and willing to accept the chance and consequences of failure. Most important, I was determined to make this work. Now what?

"Let's start with my favourite skill. Any ideas what that might be?" Sam asked.

Mike's hand shot up like a grade one know-it-all.

"Problem solving. That's it, isn't it?"

We all chuckled along with Mike. The 'one in three' guy did serve a purpose.

"That's right, Mike. If there were no problems we wouldn't need entrepreneurs or managers of any kind. Big rewards gravitate to the problem solvers, not just the idea men. If you start out as a one-person operation you'll have no choice. There'll be no room for procrastination and no chance of delegation. By definition, all problems will be yours. That's actually easy at first, especially during the honeymoon period when you're in the afterglow of the start-up. If you're on your own for too long, maybe you picked the wrong opportunity.

"Once you start building your team the problems increase in number and in difficulty, and, believe me, you still have ownership. A real entrepreneur thrives on the challenge. My most memorable years were in my first company, a partnership with my brother-in-law that hadn't been planned. His father had started the business, kept it small and profitable, but died of a heart attack with no warning at sixty. We built the business steadily over ten years from six employees up to two hundred and fifty. Along the way I learned most of the things that we'll discuss this week. Overall, It was just plain fun — stressful, demanding, exhausting, frightening, but always fun. Trying new machinery, expanding into new markets, finding new suppliers, whatever we wanted to try. We had no preoccupations, no inhibitions, and a blank canvas regarding where we could take the business. It's critical to find what you like and do it. At the same time, those things that you don't like, well they have to be done too, just as promptly and just as well as the good stuff. There is no better example than an owner-operator sharing in the workload of cleaning up a mess.

"Early in our careers one of our customers, a jean company, returned 500,000 branded leather labels. The company had been buying from six different sources, including us. Some of the sources had been using scrap leather. The customer's own standards had been all over the map, which had caused them to tighten down. There was a lot of money at stake for our small business. After a heated discussion they agreed to accept the labels back if we re-sorted them into consistent groupings, subject to their approval. It was a dog's breakfast. Almost anything had been acceptable up to that point, different shades of leather, different depths of branding, different shades of branding, different thicknesses of leather — the variety was overwhelming, at least when you tried to categorize them.

"It took six of us three weeks to try and sort them all. I worked alongside the other five every day, with my fingers crossed and my heart in my throat, but I never let anyone know my fear. The camaraderie built during those weeks was immeasurable. There were daily jokes at my expense, of course, but I got my share in too. What I learned about working within my own company was invaluable, from quite a different perspective. I was the cheerleader throughout, outwardly confident that we would be able to send all of the labels back. No one else believed it. Neither did I. At the end the customer sent their quality control manager to inspect and he approved the return of all but 2,000. I went out and bought a case of wine and the whole plant celebrated. I was vindicated and none of our staff ever found out that I didn't expect the customer to take any of the labels back. You cannot replace team building experiences like that. We had many of them. Remember, every problem is an opportunity.

"I never knew what a day would bring. My office was a revolving door of people coming in with problems to discuss and resolve. Most days I thrived on the challenge. I loved it. Even better, I found that I had a knack for anticipating problems. The more you anticipate issues the more likely you are to avoid them. It's a huge asset when you're growing and building systems."

There was a hesitation around the room. You could feel doubt creeping back in.

So I asked Sam. "How did you have all the answers? How will we have all the answers?"

Sam smiled. "Of course I didn't have them all, and you won't either. A major part of the solution has to be for you to understand as many aspects of your operation as possible. As we grew my partner and I learned how to do every job along the way. When people brought in problems we had a basic under-standing of what they did. That's one advantage of building and growing a business — you grow with it. It's difficult to gain the same insight into an established entity. Next you have to be a good listener. You have to take the time to understand your staff's concerns, which may be different than yours. Finally, you have to ask a lot of questions, which is a natural role for most entrepreneurs. You see, the person often knows the answer if you ask the right questions. Remember Socrates? He taught through questions. And finally you have to be confident and show confidence in your staff. Decisions require authority, never uncertainty.

Big business creates rigid systems as an alternative to this kind of interaction between owner-operator and employee. To me, that leads to mediocre results and lost opportunity. I believe that a better alternative is to limit the size of the operation to two hundred employees or less. That's been done quite successfully based on the premise that this is the optimum size of a firm. A few larger companies have limited the size of their various divisions based on the same logic. The auto parts sector, which feeds into a larger assembly line production, has done this very successfully. Size of operation is another topic for later."

That seemed to be enough for today. Sam had picked two hour sessions for a reason. He could see that we had already absorbed as much as possible, so he sent us off to the Deli-Caf.

CHAPTER SEVENTEEN

More about the Kellys

I had a feeling that the sessions at the Deli-Caf would change now that we knew about Jennifer. Surprisingly she was there again that night and immediately gravitated towards Grace. Terry was more subdued than normal. Mike didn't come over that night so there were just the four of us. I thought that I should bring Cheryl in to meet them all, maybe on the weekend.

I was sitting on one of the leather chairs taking to Terry while Grace and Jennifer sat at a table. It was my first chance to talk to him alone since I'd met Jennifer.

"Jennifer seems really nice." I started.

"She's doing well now, but she struggled with depression since our last daughter was born. That's really why I know Sam so well. It's been tough on all of us, but Sam and Robin have taken it hard. Their girl has an MBA and spent several years working for Research in Motion. She was riding high, working for a powerhouse that was taking off and doing so well we postponed having a family. We even discussed my becoming 'mister mom,' and I would have done it, but once she had our daughter she decided to take the full maternity leave. Before you knew it we had two more, she had been out for over six years, and RIM was focused on new graduate talent. Anyway, she couldn't go back. If she had gone back after each pregnancy they would have kept her position, but she didn't."

Jennifer looked over. I'm sure she realized we were talking about her, but she appeared to be unfazed.

Terry went on. "Sam has been fantastic. My original idea here was pretty basic and probably would have flopped. He had the idea for the conversation area and the computers. He got Jen working on the blog and the new products of the week. He's taught me a lot. That's why I pushed you to work with him. Your dad clued me in that you needed a change. Jen is capable of more, but she is happy. I'm just glad to be back together. We'll see where it goes from here."

I was feeling nostalgic and said so.

"Hard to believe that so many years have gone by and all those summers have passed since we cruised the lake. The all-powerful 'they' who say things say you never make friends quite the same way that you do when you're young. Maybe it's true. Coming here every night sure is comfortable. I'm glad for you that Jennifer's back. Thanks for introducing me to Sam. I think it's going to change my life. He's quite a guy."

Grace and Jennifer were still talking. I knew that Cheryl would like them both when they all met. That was up to me.

Then Jennifer and Grace stood up. It was time to leave. Terry locked up and we headed to our cars.

As Jennifer and Terry were walking away, hand in hand, I heard her say:

"Did you know that Grace used to be a graphic artist working for RIM? She was there when I was. She wanted to go back and do an MBA before she got pregnant. Sound familiar?"

She sounded happy. Old friends, new friends — the sharing with friends was cathartic.

CHAPTER EIGHTEEN

Planning and Control

Four days left.

Nothing but detail and dogma on the horizon. Even Mike was into it now. Once again, Sam was ready to roll.

"Yesterday was about action: making things happen and solving problems to keep things moving. Today is about control: planning, strategy, time management, negotiation, and assessment. These aren't qualities that most people identify with entrepreneurs, but I do! The giants on the extreme right side of the curve may get away with relying on others just based on the brilliance of their innovation, but don't confuse inventors with entrepreneurs. Most of you are small business operators obsessed with independence. If you only retain one thing today it better be 'know your numbers!' If you know nothing about accounting, take a course. I don't want you to be bookkeepers, but you have to understand the numbers. If you can read a balance sheet and track your major assets and liabilities you'll always know where you stand. No self-respecting entrepreneur can wait for an accountant to tell them how he or she is doing six months after their year end.

"Who can even wait until year end anyway? Cash flow doesn't lie. If you're short of cash you're either underfinanced, selling too cheap, not collecting fast enough, carrying too much inventory, or your expenses are too high. Regardless, you need to find the reason and adjust quickly. Not knowing is a poor excuse for sinking a business, but one that a lot of would-be entrepreneurs rely on. Cash flow is one of the early indicators that will guide you."

Thank God I had taken basic accounting in high school and knew my way around an Excel spreadsheet. I'd better revisit both. Maybe I should add accounting for small business to my online training program. And on he went.

"Remember, initially you are the business. Time is your biggest limitation. Action is your responsibility. Business people are lucky today. There are some good computer programs out there for budgeting and planning. You know them better than I do. Build at least four alternative sets of projections. That gives a great framework for assessing your progress. Make payback your criteria for spending decisions. If an investment in equipment can save enough money to pay for itself in short time, it should be a no-brainer. If it takes forever, forget it. The same thing applies for new hires. Payback is the key to controlling your costs, spending effectively, and re-investing in your business. Entrepreneurs who are preoccupied with creating something without regards to costs generally end up passing on their business to someone for a fraction of what it cost them.

"As for planning, it's not difficult to vary your assumptions and look at the implications using a computer spreadsheet program. You need to have a downside plan, two versions of your most likely plan, and an upside plan, all fully vented. Most of you should take your first plan and make that the upside version because we're all too optimistic — human nature. Looking at alternative scenarios is the key to understanding the business you're about to create. You're doing this exercise for you. There's an old idiom that says that most projects take twice as long, cost twice as much, and make half the profit that you think initially. Unfortunately this is true more often than not. With experience, projections improve dramatically. At the beginning use others as a sounding board, and if you have to go to a bank, never show your plans until you know they'll stand up to scrutiny. Remember the bank will love to see your downside plan and how you propose to handle it. Just having one adds to your credibility."

Sam grabbed his water bottle and chugged half of it down. There was a lot to digest, but most of it made sense. At least the interruption allowed us to ask a few questions.

Grace was anxious. "Sam, how do we know our costs with certainty? Or our revenues for that matter. I've done personal budgets but I've always had some history to go on."

Sam was patient.

"I know this can be overwhelming, but it is crucial. The process forces you to establish a realistic strategy. It makes you look at several scenarios, good and bad. Usually it shows you your vulnerability and makes you move at a realistic pace. But it is entirely based on assumptions. There is no choice. There is no such thing as planning with certainty. At the beginning that's all you have going for you."

Then he wrote a single word on the board underlining the first three letters:

*Ass*ume.

"You must have heard the old adage. The word 'assume' makes an 'ass' of 'u' and 'me.' Regardless, assumptions are the foundation of all projections. One set of assumptions *is* reckless. For a pessimist on the left side of our curve, the project will die then with their negative assumptions. For the rest of you optimists, don't rely on your first guess. Refine it, question it, and defend it. Be your most severe critic and think about how you could handle the downside. One warning: make realism temper your enthusiasm but don't lose your drive. You are the problem solver and these are just potential problems. Fear and worry are just anticipations of problems to be solved. Harness that fear and use it for motivation."

Grace still looked concerned. We had both done several budgets. I was comfortable with mine. As long as I could get the initial contract with my current employer, my revenues were conservative and my costs were predictable. Her budget was more complex and more outside her experience. She had already vented it on Terry since he had a storefront. We had both done one downside scenario, but now we would have to do others. Thank God for Excel.

Sam reverted to his agenda. He was pushing ahead to get back on schedule.

"That's enough about planning and numbers. Don't get agitated. They're tools to help you, not a requirement on their own. Planning should provide comfort and a framework, not added stress. With experience comes more certainty and better projections, but never relax, you will always need a downside version. Let's talk about negotiation. Grace, you've already started into this on your lease. How's that going?"

I knew that Grace was feeling better about her lease.

"Surprisingly well. The landlord's more flexible than I expected. He's agreed to include a phase in a rent structure over three years, a first right of refusal should he decide to sell the building, and a notice clause allowing either party to terminate on six months' notice. I feel much better."

Then Sam asked, "Tell me, Grace, why did you need the notice clause?"

She hesitated, then smiled. "When I was doing my plan I accepted that I could fail. I won't let myself, but it could happen. Since the landlord wanted my personal covenant I needed a way to cut my losses. I suppose that's downside planning."

"Exactly," said Sam. "But let's take this further. Negotiation is considered an art, a game of chess to be enjoyed, a war game to be sure, but not a war. Often you need to build an ongoing relationship with the other party; perhaps a customer, a supplier, an employee, or a landlord. What do you think the key elements in a negotiation are?"

Mike was first. "You have to be tough. You can't get pushed around!"

Sam needed Mike but still winced at his predictability.

"Right, Mike. You can't get steamrolled, but how do you prevent that?"

I took a turn. "Preparation. You have to know what's important to you and you have to understand what's important to the other side."

Grace chimed in. "You can't steam roll your adversary, either. If you want an ongoing relationship both parties need to feel happy with the result."

Sam was nodding.

"Absolutely. To put it in the vernacular, 'you have to know when to fold them and know when to hold them.' But, you can over prepare. I once had a partner who pre-negotiated with himself. That was his preparation. Along the lines of 'I can give up this, they can give up that, he'll do this, I'll do that, etc., meaning we'll end up here so I'll just offer that.' He was a poor negotiator. He conceded things upfront that he didn't have to do and he assumed that the other party would give up things that they wouldn't. He often made the other side angry and generally ended up worse off than need be. Why? Because he never understood that negotiation is a process that has to evolve. A good negotiator appears to reluctantly give up things that don't matter to him, concedes on certain issues that are critical to the other side, and never fails to get the things that are vital to his side. If the last two are at cross purposes, a deal may not be possible, but usually it is. And you have to be flexible. Negotiation is also a revelation to both parties and you have to be able to react to changing circumstances."

Mike asked. "What's the worse negotiation you ever made Sam?"

That took Sam back. "Why Mike, that might be the best questioned you've asked yet. Let me see, there've been quite a few that I regret. Oh I know, I think it's the mortgage I negotiated back in the summer of 1980. None of you have experienced anything like the high rates of inflation in the late seventies and early eighties, but I have a feeling that you will soon enough. It's easier for governments to increase revenue and pay back debt in inflated dollars. Watch out for it.

"Anyway, in the summer of 1980 my partner and I were negotiating to buy a much larger industrial building, over 100,000 square feet. Our business wasn't quite ready for it, but the building had been on the market for some time so we got the seller down to a good price. The other side was a foreign investor who was moving the operation and just wanted out of the building. We were consolidating from three much smaller buildings into this one and we would still have room for growth. In my wisdom, when we were right down to the short strokes of the deal, I decided to try and recoup our moving costs. I asked them for a six month interest-free mortgage. Interest rates were around 12 percent at the time. They agreed, on the condition that we must have a lender confirmed to take out their short-term mortgage. No problem, our bank would do that, the new mortgage would be a five-year term beginning in six months, *but* the interest rate would not be set until we drew down the funds to payout the seller. Do you see a problem shaping up here? That six months was the most explosive period for interest rates you can imagine and we ended up stuck with a mortgage rate at 19 percent for five years. It was a big lesson for me."

Everyone, including Sam, laughed at his expense. He didn't seem to mind. He talked about his mistakes as enthusiastically as did about his success. It really wasn't about the money for him. It was all about the game.

Sam shifted back into storytelling mode.

"My most frustrating dealings have been with the banks. It used to be a negotiation. They have always had the leverage, but there was some give and take. The banks really cared about small business in those days. Now they're preoccupied with the bigger and easier profits they can make elsewhere. It's a crucial restriction on entrepreneurs right now and it's getting worse. When I first started I was right out of school. My business finance professor drilled into me that we shouldn't agree to personal guarantees. So when the bank asked, I said no. Twenty three years old with no business experience and I said no! My answer was 'you're being well paid for the loan, and the only way you won't get paid back is if we have a depression, and that's your risk not mine.' How cheeky was that. Anyway, over the years we borrowed millions of dollars in that first business and never had personal guarantees. That's not going to happen for you. All banks insist on them now."

Grace had already experienced that and I'd been forewarned by Terry. It was scary.

"Perhaps the biggest problem with the banks has been that their personnel changes so often and you have to rebuild your relationship virtually from scratch. That's usually not the case with customers or suppliers, at least not as frequently. Probably the riskiest thing I did in a bank negotiation was about ten years ago We were doing a fairly large land development and were in the middle of an important funding negotiation with our bank. In the midst of the negotiation with an impending deadline, the bank switched us to a higher approval level. The fellow arrived at our office with a file about us that was two feet thick. We had been clients for over thirty years. Then he proceeded to ask us questions as if we had just walked in as new clients. I literally threw him out of our office and told him to come back when he had read the file. My language was a little more colourful. He was a V.P. of the bank.

"My partners were furious at me, and rightly so. The next morning I got a call from the banker to apologize, which I gratefully accepted and reciprocated. After that we got along very well. Both of us had learned something. I don't recommend that type of risk for you. But I do stress that you should be firm and fair with your negotiations with all parties and if they do break down in anger, make sure you mend those relationships. Anger, in business as in life, should not be allowed to happen, but like every other problem that mistake is an opportunity. People understand anger. They are much less tolerant of a grudge. A wise man used to say 'there is no face in business,' which means you should not show your emotions. Good advice that I did not always follow.

"Realistically the bank may not be an option for new businesses. Funds from family members or friends are often the source of start-up funding. If you do this make sure to document these loans from day one. If you are successful you'll be surprised how these loans will be interpreted. Venture capital is the main other option, but you have to reach a certain stage before they'll consider you, and the price is high in terms of equity. Venture capital really grew out of the tech revolution, so they expect very high returns."

It was well after five o'clock. Two hours seemed shorter and shorter. Another day with Sam was over. The everyday commitment was no big deal. My list was overflowing.

CHAPTER NINETEEN

Planning a Change of Pace

In contrast, the routine of going to the Deli-Caf every afternoon *was* becoming tedious. Emotions were riding high. Some serious life decisions had been made there in the past week about careers, business, and relationships. Sam was at the root of it all and he was still loading us up with facts, close to information overload. In the mist of all the unexpected developments, he had lost some of his mystique the last couple of days. After all, he had a wife and a daughter and worried about them both, just like the rest of us. But he was still the closest thing I had ever met to a business guru. Without any doubt, he had earned our respect. How did a stranger have so much influence in such a short time?

On top of all these emotional developments, the weather was spectacular, the lake was warm and inviting, and we were all eager to get out to our respective cottages. Terry and Jennifer were just back together, so I'm sure they had better things to do than wait for us to come back from class. In any case, they were there waiting for us that night just like every other.

I decided we needed a change. It was time my lives here intersected and that Cheryl was brought into the picture with my friends, new and old alike. We had already discussed having everyone out to the cottage for a barbecue. Since it was supposed to rain on the weekend, I made the executive decision that it had to be the next night. Cheryl hadn't even met Terry since his parents had sold the marina and moved away from the lake before we were married. It hit me that I really didn't know much about Grace or her family. Everyone accepted the invitation. Mike was the most surprised when I included him, but how could I not? He was as much a part of the last two weeks as any of us. Possibly I should have included Sam and Robin, but thought better of it. Maybe next week when this was all behind us.

My invitation seemed to give everyone a lift. Grace and Jennifer were offering to bring whatever, from salads to salmon to steak. Terry promised pies from the Deli-Caf. Not sure what Mike would bring. At that point I made the mistake of saying that in the heat I would enjoy a beer. Mike just happened to have a twelve pack in the car, on ice, in a cooler. The girls had one each. Mike, Terry, and I had two. Not enough to do damage, other than burning ear syndrome courtesy of my mother when I got home late, but the alcohol was enough to take the stress out of the moment.

It wasn't long before the talk turned to Sam. Loose lips could be revealing. I started it.

"Jen, tell us what kind of a father Sam was. I mean, one thing that's made me hesitate about starting my own business is the potential impact on my family. There are only so many hours in the day. How did he deal with conflicts between business demands and family time?"

Jennifer giggled, probably not all that used to beer on a hot day when it went down so easily.

"Let me see. If you'd asked me fifteen years ago my answer would have been different. Having a problem solver for a parent can be tough. Once we got to be teenagers, we thought he was too controlling. The need to resist made us stronger. When we were young he was there, a lot more than you might think with all the businesses he had. Now that I'm a parent I have a better idea how they handled it. Everything else was secondary, no time for clubs or recreation. Family movies, summers at the cottage, and ski trips filled up whatever free time that Sam had. Somehow we always had winter and summer family vacations together. I know now that Sam insisted on it and worked long hours before and after so we could build family memories.

"There was some business travel, but almost every night Sam put the three of us to bed. He came home early and was there for dinner. What I didn't know until I was older was that once we were in bed he went back to work. It might have been easier for him now because he would have been able to work at home. Sam loves to communicate and he prefers to write and answer at his convenience. In that sense and several others, he's a renaissance man. He's the proverbial generalist and he knows so many things. Has he told you about his book? Don't get him started on trivia. He loves his computer and has thousands of emails on his laptop because he won't delete any correspondence — he might need it later. He does Sudoku every night before bed and he still loves sports. Has he had you chipping golf balls yet? Sam's pretty much the real deal. He has a million ideas that drive you crazy when you're a kid and catch your interest when you're an adult looking for change. They have a great marriage, but he doesn't deserve all the credit for that. They're pretty much a package, true alter egos in a good way. We had a pretty idyllic childhood most of the time but it was usually his way on his schedule. As we hit adolescence there were more conflicts. Maybe that happens in every family, but the business seemed to be more of a drag in those years. All three of us thought that he put in too many hours, but look at me now.

I guess the biggest compliment that I can give the two of them is that all three of us, my brother, my sister, and I, are independent. We can stand on our own two feet, even though they're always looking over our shoulder ready to help, maybe just a little too willing with advice. Did I mention he loves his family unconditionally, especially his grandchildren? Just one more thing the two of them agree on. My only real criticism of my parents is that they always made marriage look so easy, and it's not."

Terry winced at that. His emotions were still pretty raw where Jennifer was concerned. He then offered his own perspective on his father-in-law.

"Sam's not a saint and he's the first to admit it. I attended his sessions every day, just like you, to help me get started here. Sam almost celebrates his mistakes in business and in life because he learns as much from his failures as his successes. It's one of the things I enjoyed most about his course. He really does relate his failings with as much enthusiasm as he does his triumphs. All these factors that make the perfect entrepreneur aren't about him. They're a composite of people he's observed over the years. None of us have it all. There are few superstars in business, in sports, in entertainment, or in life. Some of it comes easy, some never comes at all. Sam knows he's not on the far right of that graph, but he's damn sure that he's not on the left side. All he asks is that we learn what we can and try our best. That's his life philosophy as well. Keep an open mind and try your best. That's good enough for me."

Grace was looking a little teary eyed, Jennifer was looking lovingly at Terry, and Mike was looking longingly at the last two beers. It was time for me to leave. So I did — there was boat driving on the horizon and plans to make for the next night.

CHAPTER TWENTY

It's All about Team

Three days left.

Sam had settled into his new routine, determined to drag us into full scale entrepreneurship on his schedule, which meant picking up the pace even more.

"So we've got you making things happen, solving problems, planning, negotiating, assessing your results, anticipating future problems, watching your numbers, and more. I guess we'd better start getting you some help. Today we're going to discuss team building and partnership. Entrepreneurs have to build a team and they often have partners. Building a team and keeping it has never been more difficult. Changing jobs has become the norm. People expect several shifts in their jobs over their careers, including working for a variety of employers. Individuals in their quest for advancement doubt themselves for not moving around, equating change with experience. If you want to keep pace with the growth of your company as CEO you have to spend time on recruiting. This is one where you should not delegate.

"Staying with one company for life was once the standard in North America and a major aspect of corporate and personal philosophy in Japan and Korea. Such loyalty may be in danger of becoming passé in the current global economy. Large companies in North America seem to take this in stride. Mobility within the work force has a cost, but it fits their modular structure of interchangeable staff. For small independent operations, the job creators, this is a nightmare. As a new entrepreneur, replacing staff is about to become one of your most frequent problems. Investment in people is hard to sustain when they consistently abandon you for greener pastures. Payback on training new personnel is in decline from premature staff turnover, a change which could compromise the willingness and ability of small business owners to focus on growth and job creation, a negative trend for the economy. Rampant turnover may lower growth expectations for small business owners and weaken job creation in critical geographic and cultural areas.

"Despite this societal preoccupation with changing employers, don't give up on your employees in frustration if they resign. As difficult as it may be, don't take it personally. Sometimes you can change their mind by listening. In the business we inherited with six employees, the first person that we hired ourselves was very young, a recent high school graduate who didn't enjoy college. He grew along with us and became our production manager. Ten years later he announced that he was quitting so he could accept a job with one of our fringe suppliers. Behind closed doors we were furious and hurt. It felt personal. Somehow we sucked up our emotions and held a going away party for him at my partner's house. Over a beer he told me that the real reason he was quitting was that the pressure of running our growing production was too much stress. He still liked the company. By the time we had several more drinks we had defined a new role for him in product development which proved to be critical in the ongoing growth of our company, one of the keys to our innovation. He outlasted me in the company, staying on long after we sold it.

"Picking the right people is essential and starts with assessing your personal weaknesses. You want people that complement your philosophy, embrace your business strategy, *and* supplement your skills. When you're hiring, remember our graph representing the normal distribution of entrepreneurial skills. Based primarily on these attributes and related skill factors, there really are people who thrive either in the culture of a small company or alternatively much prefer a large one. Many of these opposite types will flounder in the alternative environment. Those that prefer a small company atmosphere like to be busy, thrive on multi-tasking, welcome a little chaos, enjoy job sharing, seldom watch the clock, and most of all need to be part of a team. They can also be disorganized and prone to procrastination. That's where your team leadership comes into play. The best of these are probably in the centre right side of our curve.

In contrast, large company people like structure, narrow job descriptions that clearly define responsibilities, clear cut deadlines that don't change, rigid corporate strategy that is laid out for the world to see, job security, a strong benefit package, and upward mobility within their field of expertise. The best of these are also in the centre of our curve, but somewhat on the left side. There is overlap of both types, generally among the people who can perform in either environment but simply prefer one or the other. Hire these people when you can. Governments are not the only entities that need balance. People with large company experience that enjoy a small company culture are assets. More extreme cases are further away from the centre of the curve and can't function effectively in the alternative environment. Serious entrepreneurs aren't happy working for others, especially in a large company culture. Bureaucrats will tear their hair out in an entrepreneurial setting. Remember this when you're hiring. Use the three month's trial religiously to asses this critical aspect of your employees. Their tendencies in this regard will *not* change.

"You do have advantages in building your team such as personal contact, the chance to show your gratitude, you can be accessible, you have the ability to get down in the trenches to work with them, incentives can be defined that do pay off because in a small company individual employees do influence results, you can establish a work ethic that pervades your space, you can arrange, even conduct, seminars that help your employees directly, and much more. When you set policy you can introduce it directly and receive input and feedback. Most of all, you can convey your passion for what you do, and believe me, true passion is contagious. You are the leader, the healer, the advisor, the mentor, and the father/mother confessor. Don't save all your creativity and innovation for your customers. Be creative in stimulating your staff. Remember, those that work for you should be from the right side of the curve and will react accordingly. If you want to keep them, new fresh ideas to motivate are critical.

"In the early stages of our evolution toward a staff of two hundred and fifty, we had a strong sense that an intense growth period was coming. We'd developed some meaningful new products and were opening up a larger geographical market. Our sales were about $300,000 a month in 1978. To deal with the increasing demands on management we implemented an incentive system for our top four managers plus ourselves — make sure you pay yourself! The four included our sales manager, product development manager, and two production managers. Substantial bonuses would be paid out for every incremental $20,000 in sales per month over and above the $300,000 average. Nothing happened in the first three months. Then our shipments exploded, hitting over $400,000, $500,000, $600,000, $700,000, and $800,000 in five consecutive months. It was exhilarating. The reward system was simple: all of us received an identical incentive, making team solidarity outstanding. We'd created the foundation for our future in a few short months. Remember, you can afford to be generous when the upside warrants it. Also you simply won't get as far on your own."

Mike interrupted. "I thought it wasn't about the money?"

Sam hesitated, caught off guard for a moment.

"It pretty much is for the employees, Mike. Not many people will stay in a job if they can make more elsewhere, but entrepreneurs will hold on to their dream when they're penniless."

Mike wasn't convinced but let Sam go on without comment. At least he was listening.

"As your company gets bigger you will reluctantly implement much-needed systems and structure. There will be no choice but to trust others and delegate out major areas of control and responsibility. Delegation is not an entrepreneurial strength, but it does work. If you hang around long enough you will eventually reach your own level of incompetence. One of the greatest threats to entrepreneurs is their own ambition. Driving a company larger and larger *is* an entrepreneurial trait. However, once the company passes a certain level, the satisfaction fades and you'll find that you're working for a whole range of beneficiaries other than yourself, especially the government.

"One of my strongest pieces of advice to you is don't make your business too big. Do not let your business outgrow you. The threat of a union could creep in as you grow but there is no excuse for letting that happen. In today's environment where so many labour and employment standards are set and enforced by government it's incumbent on you to treat your employees well and eliminate that possibility. Never forget that a union is a business itself and it brings a third party to the table that has no real interest in your business. They're looking for new sources of revenue in the form of dues and if you get big enough they will be calling.

"Occasionally growth works out, the owner survives the adjustment, and the company remains in the hands of the family. Most often this happens when the next generation has the interest and gets the education essential to manage the larger entity. Most entrepreneurs don't plan this far ahead or simply lack the ability and/or interest to run a large company. Frankly, in the fast-moving global economy we face today, planning for the next generation is a luxury.

"The best plan for most entrepreneurs is to sell their business and move on to another entrepreneurial situation, either a start-up or an idea that has merit but is floundering without the drive to make it work. The decision to sell your own creation is very painful — the most difficult one you will face. Many entrepreneurs can't make it and wait too long. Remember one of your strongest traits is to make things happen. That's why entrepreneurs start businesses better than managing them.

"A good analogy relates to when your kids were small and you were their first football or hockey coach. At the beginning no one could teach them more, and without you their interest in the game would never have developed. If you want them to continue to improve, you soon have to hand them on to someone more experienced, and if they want to make the big time only the best coaching will get them there. If you don't let them move ahead, you'll block their development. If you're lucky you can coach another son or daughter. The same is true for your business. The time will come when you will be the limiting factor. Before that happens it's best to sell and start something new, or if you're really perceptive level the business off while you can still handle it. This works for some, but few entrepreneurs are satisfied with the status quo."

This dilemma of selling or holding on seemed a long way down the road. But Mike was intrigued because that's when money would be made.

"That's called cashing out, isn't Sam? Have you ever sold your business?"

Sam looked downright melancholy for a moment.

"Another good question, Mike. It actually happened after I went to Korea back in 1987. We had a good run in that first business, lasting twenty years. We had built something worthwhile in manufacturing, including one of the best facilities in the industry, but I could see that we were vulnerable. After returning, having taken a hard look at what the Koreans were doing, I gave my partner the frank assessment of the downside scenario that we were facing. Point blank: 'this was a war we couldn't win.' The Koreans had modern plants and a disciplined, well-educated work force that wanted to work in our industry.

"This was not about cheap labour. It still isn't. It had become increasingly difficult to get people to do factory work here. Our society wanted to produce university graduates, not factory workers. We were at the beginning of the era that started the mass exodus of factory jobs to the Far East. Other countries wanted these jobs more than we did. What was allowed to happen was short-sighted. Today we have a certain percentage of our work force that is unskilled with few options to employ them. Yet we are not self-sufficient in the production of essentials such as clothing, footwear, or even food, traditional areas in which less skilled workers can function. Does this make us vulnerable? Lack of skills within a segment of our work force is a reality that is deemed politically incorrect to discuss, so potential solutions are being suppressed.

"We manufacture less and less product in North America, but we have manufactured a new economic reality through greed on the part of individuals and inaction on the part of government. Entrepreneurs have led the charge to take industry overseas, exporting markets and know-how in the process. Governments have watched, happy to mask inflation by allowing the importation of cheap goods. Individual action is often out of sync with the collective interest of a society as a whole. That's one more reason that we need effective government. As an entrepreneur you have to read trends and protect your interests. The more you can insulate your business from any and all overseas competition by selecting niche markets and localized services, the more secure you will be. It's called China-proofing your business.

"We didn't have that option, so we sold our company in 1990 in the early stages of the shift overseas. Sorry Mike, the sale didn't make us wealthy, but we did have five potential buyers and three actual bids, which allowed us to get all of our built up retained earnings out of the company and move on to other opportunities. It was a gut-wrenching decision, but it was right. Within five years the industry was in serious decline and within ten years it was totally decimated. While I often think how fortunate we were to have been that perceptive, it was one of the most painful decisions I have ever made. I still have regrets and resentment that we couldn't live out our working life further refining and improving that first business. The joy has never been quite the same. However, please don't live in denial. There will come a time in your life when selling your business is the right decision. Don't bury your head in the sand and miss that opportunity. Nothing lasts forever!

"So don't allow yourself to get so attached that you can't sell. Sometimes this is easier said than done. When you do sell, don't expect to stay on as an executive for long. The buyer will probably be a larger entity. They grow by acquisition, not start-ups. You won't like the new subculture, and once they've picked your brain, they won't like you. There are exceptions, but most of us can't bear to watch the assimilation of our creation. Integration means change. Strategies are different. Your team will be dismantled. Get your reward in the selling price. A fat employment contract may entice you, but it will likely end prematurely or you will spend years as a frustrated indentured labourer for the money. Big corporations like earn outs, but if you negotiate hard and they want your company badly enough, you can avoid them. Selling is the exit plan so get your money up front, stay for the shortest possible time, and move on to your next venture."

Sam was full of surprises. I hadn't expected advice about an end game. We had just made the decision to go ahead with the start-up. We were all surprised by his candour, but he didn't wait for us to absorb the practicality of his advice before moving on to his next topic.

"Let's talk about partnerships for a while. Many entrepreneurs start out in a partnership or find themselves in one early in their careers. It's partially a comfort thing. It's tough to be the one at the top on your own with no one to share the stress and pressures. Sharing the burden and the risk is tempting, a way to hedge your bets. Besides, you can only lean so hard on your spouse. My first partnership was enduring. We grew up together in business, forging ideas and experiences we had shared with no one else. We remain partners in several ventures to this day.

"That's simply not the norm! Most partnerships don't end well. The entire basis of starting a company is to grow it and mature with it. Very few partners grow and mature at the same rate. The main way that partnership works is if you have different skills and the nature of the business allows you to split responsibilities on a fairly even basis. This arrangement requires unconditional trust, which is fraught with potential problems. The alternative is that one partner ignores the fact that he or she has matured further and faster than their associate, is prepared to disregard the divergence, and assumes an unofficial lead role. This happens often and it can work for some time. However, effectively, one partner is subsidizing the other and that can't last indefinitely.

"Just as you should plan for the sale of your business, you should also have a mechanism in place that provides for the breakup of the partnership, if not because the relationship becomes unworkable, at least in case there is a death or disability. The most common arrangement is some kind of buy-sell arrangement. I prefer an agreement providing for third party evaluation or market evaluation to determine the transfer price, but generally these agreements include a shotgun clause whereby one party sets a price and the other elects to either buy out or sell to the first partner at the price offered. This puts the onus on the first party to name a fair price, intended to be market or higher. Unfortunately I have seen some bizarre results from these types of agreements.

"The most unusual case I can remember involved two partners and their families. The second generation of one of the families was very active in the business. Their father died first, but because his son and daughter were active in the day-to-day operation they retained the shares by agreement with the original partner. The buy-sell shotgun arrangement stayed in place between the two families for years. When the second original partner died his family had no interest in continuing. The son of the first partner made a very fair offer to buy the shares because he didn't want any issues between the families. What he didn't know was that two other key managers of the company had arranged for bank support and offered to buy the entire company from the second family at a 10 percent premium over his offer without even knowing what that offer was. So the second family elected to buy the son out under the shotgun clause and then sold all the shares to the management, leaving him out of a job. At least he got a good price.

"Within five years the company was bankrupt because the buyout had been debt financed by the company, which went from being cash rich to highly leveraged. So the first warning here is that the partner you start with may not keep pace with you. The second warning is that you may end up in partnership with someone else, or even out in the street. The third warning relates to setting the price of a shotgun clause too low because you're sure the other side can't operate the company or can't come up with the funding. I have seen many companies lost over this type of greed. Don't underestimate your partner; he may want the business as much or more as you do.

"A bad partnership can kill a business just like any other toxic relationship. It diverts energy and effort away from management and is a divisive factor that destroys the team you have worked so hard to develop. Silent financial partners can even be worse since their contribution is invisible. No matter how essential outside funding is to your launch, that partner will be resented and forever labelled overpaid. Pay them a royalty with a cap and considerable upside but limit their return or you will regret it forever. An active financial partner can be an asset. Remember you must still know and understand your numbers. Unfortunately the trust relationship between active financial partners and operating/managing partners has often been abused. Just be careful who you take on. Human nature is the demon here. Partners seldom agree on how a business has evolved or who has made the most important contributions."

Finally there was a break that would allow me to ask a question.

"Sam, when you were describing the buy-sell shotgun that backfired on the second generation, that was the first time you mentioned a family business. What about partnerships with family members? How do you feel about that? A lot of small businesses involve family."

Sam hesitated before answering.

"Frankly, Tim, that's another two week course and I do give it. There are so many added complications when family are involved, but all of the issues I just mentioned still apply. Merging family and business can work. There are lots of examples, but it can also compromise both. I've seen loyalty to the point of stupidity, but I've also seen family backing that has saved many small companies. How do you fire a brother or invoke an agreement to get him out? Not easy. It really does take another course to cover all the issues involved in the family business. My advice is to treat it just like any other start-up. Do your analysis, look at the downside, and plan for it. Most people ignore the possibility that a family business can be divisive. Open discussion and planning for that possibility is constructive. Anyway, none of you are planning to take in an active family partner, are you?"

I hesitated, thinking of my dad's offer to invest, and wondered if Grace would mention her husband Doug but then reconsidered. Neither of these would be active partnerships. Mike still had no plan so none of us said a thing.

"A good alternative to a partner can be a small business consultant, but you need to find someone who has walked in your shoes. It's a role you might consider yourself once you sell your business. Consulting fills a void between projects and it may lead to opportunities. A good adviser can facilitate your needs at the bank, help you build your alternative plans, recognize developing trends, introduce you to a wealth of contacts from professionals to clients, and mentor you through the first difficult years. On the surface they are expensive, but the costs are minor in relation to what can happen with a full-scale partner, and the relationship does give you a sounding board. Another good alternative is an advisory board, either an official board of directors or an informal one, in either case made up of people you trust with relevant experience who are outside your business and personal life. You need to be able to vent to people who will help you maintain perspective."

It was hot and humid that day. Thunderstorms were forecast for later that night. I was thinking about the barbecue, hoping the storm would hold off, and savouring the thought of the beer I'd had the night before. Frankly I'd started to tune Sam out, since I had no intention of taking in a partner. By the time I realized that I had drifted off. Sam was right in my face.

"Not keeping you up, are we Tim? You know I can take your little nap one of three ways. Either you don't like consultants or my eloquence is slipping or you've had enough for today. Since Mike is still awake, I'm leaning towards you having had enough. What do you think? Probably time to leave, just two more days that you all have to show up."

CHAPTER TWENTY-ONE

Getting to Know You

Summer barbecues at the lake in July are the best: perfect weather for swimming, long days with glorious sunsets over the water, full of mindless relaxed chatter and tons of food to eat on a totally informal basis. This particular barbecue started with two shockers, at least for me. First Mike appeared with his mother, quite a distinguished white haired lady, who arrived in a lovely light blue Mercedes convertible, top down, clearly in command, with her son in the front passenger seat. Not at all what I had expected when he asked me if he could bring someone. Then Grace arrived. She was also driving, in this case an SUV, with her two daughters in the back. Those two were off and running with our three boys plus Terry and Jennifer's two daughters and son, practically before the car stopped. Cottage life makes kids more outgoing.

Grace introduced me to her husband Doug, who was still sitting in the car. We were in the midst of talking about Sam when I noticed Grace getting something large out of the back. Cheryl was helping her. At first I thought it was a cooler, but it was a wheel chair. Doug was tied to a wheel chair and I had no idea. Grace had hardly mentioned Doug except to say that he supported her on her new business. I suppose I hadn't said much more about Cheryl, but I felt guilty and insensitive. How could I have talked to Grace so often about our goals and aspirations and have no idea about this? No wonder she was so concerned about succeeding.

The rest of the night was a blur. The storm never did materialize. I spent most of the time driving the boat, taking the kids tubing and water skiing. Mike was my spotter. The highlight of the night for the kids was Mike taking a barefoot run all around the bay. His water skiing made Terry and I look like rank amateurs. The barefooting was the final straw. I had never learned how, so the kids had a new hero. Doug and Terry ran the barbecue. There was a steady stream of hotdogs and burgers supplemented by potato salad, tossed salads, coleslaw, watermelon, and then, of course, ice cream and apple pies from the Deli-Caf. I hardly had a chance to speak with an adult.

Doug was something else, clearly comfortable in his own skin, interacting with my mom and dad, joking with Terry and Mike, making Cheryl and Grace laugh so hard they cried over one of his stories, happily flipping burgers, watching the kids ski, and enjoying the whole scene. At the end of the night he had all of the kids mesmerized, telling them the legend of Tommy Whopper, the biggest fish in the lake who loved to steal food off the dock. What none of us knew was that he had orchestrated Mike to do a cannonball off the boathouse deck just when the story reached its climax and Tommy jumped back into the lake. The looks on everyone's face when they heard the big splash were priceless. By that time it was dark and time for everyone to leave. It was only later in bed that Cheryl gave me new insight into my two classmates.

"Your mom really hit it off with Ruth Reynolds. Apparently they've both been coming here for most of their lives and have some mutual friends. It didn't take long for her to lose her reserve and open up about her son. Mike's life has been much different than you thought. He's the only child of older parents. Mike was diagnosed with ADHD when he was seven, put on Ritalin when he was eight, and turned to pot and worse when he was sixteen. He and his parents were at loggerheads for years, definitely all through his teens. Ruth described him as fiercely defiant. At the peak of their conflict Mr. Reynolds died abruptly of a heart attack, three months after selling his business so he could spend more time with Mike and his wife. That pushed Mike right over the top, he was into coke, acid, mushrooms, and God knows what else. Apparently he went into a serious depression before he finally accepted treatment. That's still his mother's major worry, that he'll slip back into a depression from which he never recovers. The sessions with Sam are the first thing that he's stayed with for years without the help of drugs. Mike has a huge trust fund but right now he thinks he has to be his father. Mike needs to be an entrepreneur, more than any of you. He desperately needs it. Ruth spoke to Sam about it yesterday. He was crushed; said that he'd been tough on Mike but Ruth feels that's been a good thing. Evidently he talks about you, Sam, and Grace all the time."

It was so obvious now. Mike had a hard time in class, fidgeting off and on, even getting out of his seat and moving around the room, he couldn't concentrate, day dreamed, and even fell asleep. Every once in a while he'd blurt out an answer. I made fun of him — the kid who thought everything came easily, the boy who was sure that entrepreneurship ran in his veins, and the awkward young guy who was too lazy to work for what he wanted. What did I know? What a putz! First Terry had huge problems, then Grace, and now Mike.

Cheryl continued to fill me in on the conversations that took place when I was out on the boat.

"I really like Grace and Doug. I guess you knew about the accident but you didn't tell me. She's been holding things down for three years running a graphics business out of the house, designing websites and picking up whatever creative work she can. They're both graphic artists, so as Doug recovered, he's gradually been taking that over. There hasn't been enough work for both of them. She interviewed everywhere she could over the past year, but with all the cutbacks taking place and being out of the workforce for seven years she can't get anything. That's why she came up with the good yarn idea. She's desperate to find something that generates enough income and has a back office for Doug to keep doing the web design. I know that Sam discussed entrepreneurship of necessity versus entrepreneurship of opportunity, but you're way out in left field here. Grace and Doug really need this to work. Their self-respect, their financial future, and probably their marriage, they're all on the line. Mike needs it just as much. This is a healing process for him, actually for all of them; for Terry and Jennifer, Doug and Grace, and for Mike. Are you sure you belong in this class?"

As I pulled Cheryl into my arms, I was sure. For me, learning from Sam was all about gaining perspective: on life, on determination, on friendship, and most of all on myself. I knew that I would never be the same; never again be complacent about my abilities, never again squander my opportunities. It was indeed the time of my life when I needed to start making things happen.

CHAPTER TWENTY-TWO

The End Is in Sight

Two days left.

Nothing was said about the night before. Mike seemed oblivious to any change in our perception of him. Grace was her usual pleasant self, with no indication that her challenges were greater than anyone else. Sam was simply the Everyday Entrepreneur, preaching his insight yet another day. If he had any reservations from his conversation with Mrs. Reynolds, he was no more deferential to Mike than ever, still riding his essential 'one out of three' student for every inane response. I was impressed with all of them; this little congregation was quite a microcosm of the modern entrepreneurial world. Incredible, the life lessons I was learning in such a short time. Regardless, we were on a tight schedule to finish so Sam got underway as soon as we sat down. He started with a question.

"I know tomorrow's our last day, but we basically added an extra day I hadn't planned on. Can the three of you come in for a short session on Sunday afternoon? I know it's not one of the days I made you sign on for, but I need the time to wrap things up properly."

What were we going to say? He wasn't charging us anything. Frankly I don't think any of us were ready for his sessions to end. Grace summed it up for all of us.

"Sam, if you need more time, I'll be here. I want the benefit of your wisdom."

Mike and I nodded our agreement. One extra day with Mr. Everyday was set, so Sam started out with more intensity than ever.

"Today we're going to cover several of the elements that most people *do* identify with entrepreneurs: creativity, innovation, and relationships. All of these are key to building your market and your customer base. How many times have you heard 'sales are the lifeblood of a company?' Well here's another saying to consider: 'salesmen are like halfbacks. They get the glory, but they go nowhere without the rest of the team.' You have to be the quarterback and the playing coach. Sit back and design the plays, be creative and innovative, but you also have to be part of the execution. You personally have to interact with everyone in the game: your customers, your suppliers, your employees, your competitors, and anyone else that comes into play. Nice sports analogy, don't you think? Notice it ties together team and leadership.

"Relationships are the key to execution, and they take work. Building sound bonds means setting your ego aside. It means being willing to talk to corporate CEOs and floor workers alike and feeling comfortable with both. It means listening to all of them with respect and asking relentless questions. If you ignore any of them you will be out of touch with some element of your business. Above all, don't ever allow yourself to become disconnected from your market. The minute you start to take your customers for granted you're vulnerable. In today's global marketplace you're vulnerable anyway. When Robin was learning to drive a car, her father told her 'to drive like everyone else is drunk.' He was ahead of the times on defensive driving. So be defensive in your business — treat all your customers like you could lose them tomorrow. Competitors will keep knocking on the door but you have the relationship and the inside track to stay ahead of them. Don't squander that advantage!

"In my first business I was able to develop a unique relationship with what became our best customer. The company was a bastion of quality but very old school in their approach. Their offices felt like a museum of the industry, stuffy and traditional, filled with antiques, but in a good way that's less acceptable today. Their image was an enduring testament to stability, reliability, and quality. The first time I approached them when I was twenty-three their purchasing agent told me point blank that 'you will never sell to this company.' I didn't hear the word *never*, a true entrepreneur *never* does, accept as a challenge. I was already working on how I was going to sell them. The answer came much later through a combination of creativity and innovation. Do you know the difference?"

Mike, who was pacing at the back of the room, as he was prone to do, blurted out, "Aren't they the same thing?"

Sam gave Mike a look before he explained himself, a little more patiently.

"They are to some degree, Mike, but in my business, to help me manage my time, I distinguished between them to establish different goals. For me creativity is about image and marketing while innovation is all about product and methods. Creativity is the cornerstone of shameless self-promotion, which is essential for every independent business operator. Swallow your pride and get used to it! The distinction allowed me to set clear goals in both of these key image-related areas without blurring the objectives. My first goal was to create the image that my company was an expert in our product line, which was providing a raw material for secondary manufacturers, our customers. We were a primary manufacturer. Initially we achieved this through relentless trial and error, striving to make products that none of our competitors could. If necessity is the mother of invention, than speculation is the mother of innovation. Eventually we did become the expert, a fact which nurtured many creative ideas to promote our image. Through innovation in product design and manufacturing process, we did make products that no one else had. Once we created the image highlighting our innovation we became dominant in our niche market. It took ten years to break down the barriers at that largest potential customer, but we did.

"My relationship with that same purchasing agent became so close that in his old style of operating, he insisted that I meet him every Friday morning at 6:30 at those same historical offices to plan for the upcoming weeks, discuss new product needs, and get orders. Never forget to ask for the order. He would have the coffee made. The place was dark and a little creepy with all those artifacts mixed in with modern technology. No one else showed up for another hour. Eventually he would hand me their internal computer print outs showing their production schedule and their material requirements for several weeks. The pinnacle of the relationship came when they were running a seminar program conducted by a consulting firm for all their department heads, focused on 'continuous improvement.' The program ran twice a week for three months and I was the only outsider included.

"Together he and I developed a 'just in time' inventory system that saved the customer a great deal of money, freed up working capital, and guaranteed us, the supplier, a high volume of sales with what had become our largest account. Those were exciting times, just prior to the onslaught of competition from the Far East. On one of my best days in 1985, I got a million dollar order from him, left his office at 7:30, drove thirty miles to another good account, picked up an order for $300,000 and was back in my office by 9:00."

Mike liked that narrative. "My dad used to tell me stories like that. He loved his business."

It was the first time he'd mentioned his family. Maybe last night had lifted some inhibitions after all.

Sam went on. "It was fun, no doubt about that. Every company was preoccupied with customers but there was another different relationship that I believed in and still do. We worked very hard on our relationships with suppliers. Never forget the key premise that one good supplier will help you succeed with every one of your customers. We treated all of our suppliers that way, as a valued member of our team; we preached the same philosophy to our customers. So many good ideas and innovations evolved from working closely with our key suppliers based on product and service requests from our customers. Client needs were the focus of innovation, but the suppliers were the conduit to find the way. We could rarely make things happen without input from our suppliers.

"Once you establish your reputation as an expert, customers look to you for innovation, bringing you their needs, which is your entree to the market. Relationships, creativity, and innovation have to be integrated. Developing products for which there is no market is a ludicrous waste of time and effort and a common problem for would-be entrepreneurs. Filling an established need that solves a problem is an easy sell compared to convincing someone that something new is essential. You can develop products and services in a vacuum with little success, but good relationships focus you on what is needed *and* how to find it *and* how to get your product or service to the end user."

Sam grabbed his water bottle. He was doing most of the talking that day, but he had our attention.

"When I became a land developer my ability to build solid relationships was very helpful. Development is a costly, slow process fraught with frustration for someone who has acted independently in a different business. It can be a bureaucratic nightmare, requiring uncharacteristic patience for a fast moving entrepreneur. What saved my sanity was developing solid working relationships with the multitude of professional advisors that every developer must have to meet all the reporting, study, and design requirements. Even more important was establishing an open and frank rapport with municipal staff. Understanding their culture and working within their framework was essential.

This connection didn't lead to favours but it gave me the chance to make my case on a whole range of issues based on logic. Mutual respect and understanding made the process palatable and manageable *most* of the time. Slamming the desk and ranting against the system never works. No doubt there are times when you will do just that, but keep it to yourself. Bullying doesn't work with the private sector, so why would it work dealing with government?

"The last critical relationship for a land developer, unless he chooses to build the houses as well as service the development, is his rapport with house builders. We were fortunate to build an excellent rapport with two lesser-known builders whose quality commitment matched the image we wanted for our development. Both companies grew significantly in the process of working closely with us in markets that were on the peripheral for larger conventional builders. The two came at the market from different directions, with the first company shifting from being a builder of custom homes, determined to reach into the higher volume market. The second was an up-and-coming company owned by two young brothers who were very hands on, running a tight ship, with low overheads. Their background was a lower priced, competitive market in which their low overheads allowed them to compete with higher volume efficient builders. We took a chance on them based on their knowledge and enthusiasm. It paid off."

Sam needed another sip of water. We were engaged in his story and didn't want to interrupt the flow.

"We managed to develop a trust relationship with both builders based on close co-operation and a community of interest. We carried out several projects with each, with the young brothers maturing into a sizable builder. During the process, while we all learned, both companies retained and extended their reputation as quality builders. As a result, we became perceived as a respected developer. One of the important practices we adopted in appraising a new project was to bounce all future development opportunities off our builders. They were closer to the market and without their input we would have been out of touch. As I said earlier, developing product in a vacuum is a recipe for disaster. Know your market and your access to it. For us the builder was the access. Mutual trust was the foundation of working together.

"There's one other thing I did when I started into the development game. I took my friend Bob's suggestion and studied for my real estate license right up to the broker level. If you do switch the nature of your business, taking courses can ease the transition."

Sam reviewed his notes for a minute and then resumed, switching topics as he did.

"There's one thing as entrepreneurs that you all have going for you that I didn't and I'm pretty jealous about it. Oh I'm benefitting right now, but I could really have used this one early in my career. You can thank Bill Gates and Steve Jobs, among others, for current technology. The electronic revolution has been a boon to creativity and entrepreneurship. It's barely thirty years since the fax machine came into widespread use and twenty-five since mass production of personal computers began. Now you can carry around a laptop that weighs a pound or less, for a minimal cost, that has more capacity than a mainframe Univac computer the size of a train had when I joined my first business. Software and social media offer you incredible creative tools for self-promotion. Lack of financial resources and depth in your staff won't prevent you from developing and maintaining a first-class image through your website and blog, as long as you can deliver on that image. A dedicated entrepreneur can out-shine huge companies and reach a much larger niche market in inexpensive ways. The competition is relentless, coming at you from every direction, but the opportunities are limitless. The shift towards big business, big government, and big labour might well have flattened us all without the competitive edge we get from technology.

"That brings me back to one of my favourite topics. Now, there's no excuse for not knowing your numbers. As an owner of a small company you can have your accounting system current and with you at all times, on that same laptop along with spreadsheets with all your projections for review and comparison with actuals, plus monitoring your costs, a calendar that prompts you to ensure effective time management, contact lists for all your key customers, suppliers, and professionals, email access to all of them, and the ability to balance your lives by taking all of this home to wait patiently for you while you spend time with your family. No wasted time going back to the office. You have a phone and camera with you at all times and computer access to business news and updates. Every entrepreneur has to be a generalist and wear countless hats out of necessity. Technology allows you to switch roles and access the necessary tools instantly. The revolving door that I thrived on in my career has picked up speed, but the ability to solve problems and make things happen has increased even more dramatically.

"One warning: don't lose balance! Hyper connectivity is a blessing and a curse. Use the flexibility provided by technology to improve the balance in your life, not to destroy it. A 24/7 commitment will drown you and destroy the most important relationships: friends and family. You simply have to work to live. There is no meaningful future in living to work. Dickens highlighted the issue just as the Industrial Revolution reached its peak. In 1843 he introduced the world to Ebenezer Scrooge, who remains the personification of putting work and business ahead of all else. Don't forget the lesson: once a year the story of Scrooge reminds us of the importance of balance."

Mike looked very sad at these last comments. I probably wouldn't have noticed before that day. He'd been pretty relaxed that session, staying in his seat for the most part and only blurting out the odd answer to Sam. How was he ever going to recover from his loss? Sam noticed his melancholy as well.

"You know, Mike, I did some business with your dad. He was a great guy to work with. He was very proud of you. He'd show us pictures of you barefoot skiing in the summer, doing mogul runs in the winter, and running on your cross country team. It was the first thing that came up whenever I was in his office. Your dad had balance."

That personal anecdote brought a broad smile to Mike's face, but our time was already up for the day, sooner than any of us wanted. There was no meeting at the Deli-Caf to wind down. Terry and Jennifer had gone to the city for the afternoon and wouldn't be back until the next day. Mike stood tall as we left for the night. I hadn't realized before but he must have been six foot three. Sam was a sensitive guy, maybe not right up on technology or social media, but he still knew exactly how to build relationships, even with the "one in three" guy in his class. There was one more day to go to complete our pact with Sam by showing up without fail. The last "everyday" was on the horizon.

CHAPTER TWENTY-THREE

Today Is All About You

One day left plus a short session tomorrow. The Everyday Entrepreneur was pumped.

"Today is all about you: one solitary cog in the wheel of the world economy that makes things happen. To quote James Lovell, the lunar astronaut who survived the Apollo Thirteen travesty: 'there are people who makes things happen, there are people that watch things happen and there are people that wonder what happened. To be successful you need to be a person who makes things happen.' It's the entrepreneurial self-starter side of your personality that pushes you to try. It's one of the many aptitudes that we all have in varying degrees. Remember the normal distribution we discussed and our bell curve of achievers.

"Entrepreneurs are a potent economic catalyst, the resource that puts so many other resources to work. Napoleon once referred to Britain as a 'nation of shopkeepers,' which he considered an unfit adversary for the military might of his empire. Much has been made of the emperor underestimating his main adversary. Napoleon was actually paraphrasing Adam Smith, who is considered the founder of modern economics. What Smith was referring to was quite different and described the collective will of the merchants of Britain to assert pressure on their government to push and prod the growth of their empire through trade and enterprise.

"Anyway, today is not about the general, it's about the generalist; that's you. There are so many things left to tell you and forewarn you. First and foremost, another reminder, pay yourself a fair salary. Too many people start a business and subsidize it by not paying themselves, creating a false sense of business success at the expense of personal savings. Others who have some initial success, make the opposite mistake and overpay themselves, drawing too much out of their company, putting it at risk. So pay yourself a fair salary; if you can't, your business isn't viable. Make sure you include enough for retirement savings in that remuneration package. Business success can be a fleeting experience. Keep your personal investments separate from your business investments — balance! Don't manage your personal investments. Most entrepreneurs are hands-on active investors who like to control the physical place that they invest. There's comfort in control. This makes most of us lousy passive investors when we have to sit on the sidelines and watch others make our money work for us. Search out a competent advisor and concentrate on your business.

"Manage your risk within the business by moderating it. That's why we do downside planning. Manage your risk in your personal investments with help, according to your life plan and projected needs. Remember your business is not you. It is a separate entity whose needs, at times, may well run contrary to your personal interest. Protect your personal assets. Carry adequate insurance to cover both personal and business needs. Find an advisor that you trust and put at least ten percent of your remuneration each year into separate savings outside the business no matter how much the business needs cash. Maximize your RRSP and TFSA accounts. Diversification of your assets is critical. Don't depend on future profits in your business: they may not be there when you most need them.

"Since you are the principal human resource asset of your company, invest in yourself. Take seminars, attend trade shows, travel to other markets to learn and broaden your horizons. We always invested heavily in this type of activity. Remember payback. There were no business trips that we made, shows that we attended or later exhibited in, or courses that we took where we weren't determined to get enough workable ideas or contacts to more than pay the cost. If you have the confidence and the determination to find payback, this is a no-brainer and a moderate risk. Be kind to yourself and your family — make sure you take breaks and vacations. You'll need them. Recharging your batteries is a real phenomenon."

Sam was already on his second bottle of water. Mike was pacing the room. Grace and I were writing furiously, trying to absorb but determined not to forget anything.

Sam started in again.

"There are so many ideas to convey: the need to be decisive, the importance of pride of performance, the impact of determination, the critical need to lead, the example of discipline, the power of confidence, these are all factors that will contribute to your success. They are all part of your mantra 'to find a way,' the mantra of 'how.' Your motivation will be your inspiration, what moves you to action. For me that was the fear of failure. That drove me to action much more than the desire for success. I know you want the money Mike but money alone will not be enough.

"Greed and prestige are false idols that generally break down. Greed leads to bad decisions. Collectively it leads to a bubble and a collapse that punishes everyone involved, not to mention a lot of innocent bystanders. If it looks to be too good to be true, it usually is. Never (there goes that word again) forget the linked relationship between risk and reward. If the return is unusually high, than the risk will be even higher. If the risk is particularly low than the return will be lower yet. This applies to your business decisions and your personal investment decisions. Back in 1978–1979 many professionals, particularly dentists and medical doctors, were investing in Lloyd's of London as members, in programs that personally guaranteed the underwriting of liability insurance. In effect, if there was a claim against the company, the investors/ members in that section participating in the underwriting program had to collectively pay up, no matter what the amount. This program had been extremely profitable for those who invested in the previous decade. A good friend of mine, a dentist, was looking at the investment and asked me to review the details. After reading it I asked him a simple question: 'Do you understand the meaning of unlimited liability?' When I explained things to him, he declined the investment.

"Many others did not understand the risk and went ahead. No one contemplated the huge claims related to asbestos, health claims, and pollution such as the Exxon Valdez — no one, except perhaps Lloyds, who kept recruiting new members to fund liability claims that were on the horizon. When the crap hit the fan it was a disaster for many naïve people. In some cases both husband and wife were members, wiping out all of their assets. Fortunes were lost and careers extended, all because of greed. Another friend labelled this program 'Freedom 95.'

"The reason we have corporations referred to as limited companies is because the limitation means that the liabilities of that corporate entity are limited to the assets of that company. Companies do go bankrupt when their liabilities exceed their assets. If you give a personal guarantee to a bank, that commitment overrides the limited liability and makes you liable to the bank for any shortfall of their loan. The real goal of any bank is to make sure that the bank gets paid out in preference to everyone else. As the owner-operator making things happen, it is in your interest to see the bank paid out, if you have personal guarantees. The guarantees also ensure that you won't strip the assets out of the company and leave the bank high and dry.

"Preoccupation with prestige can be more damaging than forced personal covenants, pushing you to take greater risks.

While I am a huge believer in shameless self-promotion and developing an image that helps you succeed, when your goal becomes protecting that image or worse, the personal stature that you've gained, you have taken your eye off the ball. Decisions will be made to maintain your image, not to drive the success of the business. Once they have the experience of creating a company, many entrepreneurs are able to repeat their success in a different area but some are not. As you know many of the skills required to succeed are transferable into an alternative opportunity. That ability is a great asset in today's fast-moving global economy where career change is the norm, but never take it for granted. There are one-act wonders in business as in every other field. You have to prove yourself in each new venture.

"Some people enjoy initial success due to circumstances, or a particular skill that can't be transferred. This often happens in partnerships where the combined skills of the partners create success, but on their own they can't duplicate the results. I have seen too many instances of initial success that causes a would-be mogul to fall victim to their persona as a free-wheeling entrepreneur, desperate to maintain their image, leading them to make high-risk investments only to lose their wealth. Perhaps these second-time failures are the source of the myth that you have to make a million dollars and lose a million to be a true entrepreneur. That's pure rationalization — one last desperate stretch to retrieve their mystique."

Sam could see we were fading at that point. We had covered most of the details he'd prepared.

"Hang in there. Just one quick point for today, then we can wind things up tomorrow afternoon. Get good accounting and legal advice when you're setting up your company. In fact, make sure you're aligned with good professional advisors who know and understand you from the outset. If you choose wisely, these people will be with you for the long haul, right through to your ultimate sale. They will guide you through the complexity of the

Income Tax Act, help you avoid the pitfalls of ownership, and direct you to capitalize on the benefits. This is not a place to cut costs. There are lots of young professionals trying to make partner that need up-and-coming clients that they recruit. Good advice doesn't have to be expensive. Strive to structure your company in a way that will protect the principle of limited liability. Also get good accounting advice on your share structure. It's more credible and far less costly, to have a spouse involved from the outset providing income splitting opportunities that can save you thousands of dollars over your career, than to try to revise your share structure later. And like it or not, you do need a relationship with a bank and a banker. Better to start building that relationship before you need to borrow any money.

"That has to be it for this afternoon. You must be saturated with information. Congratulations on making it here every day. Without your commitment to do that I really would have called things off. I will try and keep things short tomorrow."

Then as fast as it had started twelve days ago, the course of The Everyday Entrepreneur was over. Tomorrow would be anticlimactic.

CHAPTER TWENTY-FOUR

Is That All There Is?

Our last after class meeting at the Deli-Caf started off as a downer. All those last-minute details were overwhelming. The three of us had been sitting there in virtual silence for fifteen minutes, when Terry finally sat down. It was Saturday night so there had been a flurry of cottagers looking for the weekend specials. Business was still improving, so the environment was positive if the mood was not.

Mike spoke first.

"I'm not ready for this, am I?"

I think he echoed all of our thoughts right at that moment.

Grace tried to mollify him.

"Mike, you're the youngest. You're not married. You've got lots of time to figure this out. Look at me; I've got to make this work *now*!"

Terry and I spoke in unison.

"You will, Grace. Of course you will."

That broke the ice, especially for Mike. Everyone laughed as he said;

"Oh great, I didn't notice the two of you rush to make me feel any better."

Terry took the bait.

"Mike you *are* young. None of us had this kind of exposure at your age. Make the most of what you've learned. Take a job with someone else. You need experience more than you need money. Work somewhere that you can see Sam's advice in action. Why, you can work here for the rest of the summer if you like. It would mean early mornings with Jennifer, but she needs some help. What do you say?"

Mike was pleased. He didn't hesitate. He ran right over to Jen.

"Jen, Jen. Terry just hired me to work with you. Is that okay?"

Mike was excited but he knew who the boss was and where he would learn the most. In a matter of minutes hours were set, starting on Monday morning at three o'clock. He was ready to work at whatever they needed and he insisted that he didn't need to be paid. He wanted the experience and he wanted some responsibility. Mike had learned something from Sam, more than I would have thought possible a week ago.

"You've already been giving me free coffee and muffins this summer, that's all I need. I'll stay until Labour Day when the cottagers go home then I'll leave too. The only thing I want is a letter of recommendation provided I earn it, and I will!"

Terry was laughing.

"Didn't you learn anything from Sam? Make sure you get what you're worth. When you are on your own you can't work for nothing. Actually, maybe you can, Mike."

They finally agreed on the minimum wage for his "apprenticeship." Mike was officially an "entrepreneur in training." I could feel the excitement rising over that development. Terry and Jen were thrilled to help Mike. Everyone was pleased to see Mike so animated. While the three of them were talking about their plans over frozen caramel lattes, the new item of the week, I had a chance to talk to Grace for the first time since the barbecue.

"You should have told me about Doug. I felt like such a fool when I met him."

Grace was still looking over at Mike and his obvious joy.

"What difference would it have made? Does it matter how it happened or the nightmare that we lived through for over three years? Would you have pitied me? Neither Doug nor I want that. We've moved past all of that and now he's running our website business. More important he's got his self-respect back and he's doing good work. As long as I don't take crazy risks with Blend a Good Yarn we're in good shape. What I really needed this summer I got from you and Terry and now I'm getting more of it from Cheryl and Jennifer, even from Mike. Both Doug and I need a support group. We don't need support for our past problems, we've dealt with those. We need new friends and support from those that understand our next challenge. We need to be part of Sam's army of entrepreneurs, associated with others who are going through the same challenges that we are, people who relate to us for what we're doing not for what we can't do, not because Doug is an invalid but because he isn't. I need to be able to pick up the phone and compare notes. I need to brainstorm and come up with joint projects. I've found exactly what I need right here at the Deli-Caf and you didn't have to know anything about Doug to help me."

She hesitated, smiling as she did for a moment, before continuing.

"Sam's taught us all a great deal this summer from attendance on up. Just look at Mike. We thought he was nothing more than another smart-assed kid. You know, I picked the name for my store for the double entendre. I thought it was clever. The idea was to mix knitting and conversation, two different spins on the word yarn, if you like. But who could have spun a wild yarn like this out of a quiet two weeks at the cottage?"

CHAPTER TWENTY-FIVE

The Graduation

The last day — or was it the first?

Sam arrived late to find the three of us chattering away about our plans, with Mike by far the most enthusiastic. The Everyday Entrepreneur seemed a little hesitant but we stopped talking, as usual, focused on his first words.

"It's important that you understand the business environment you will face and the role that small independent entrepreneurs can play collectively in influencing the future. In many ways we are in uncharted economic territory. Leadership is hesitant and large entities are unwieldy. We need problem solvers on many levels. The word *entrepreneur* actually comes from a French verb *entreprendre*, which means 'to undertake.' Appropriately it's originates as a verb, an action word. Meanings of 'to undertake' include 'making a pledge to do something' and 'to set about doing.' It's a fairly basic concept implying both commitment and action, but wide varieties of people have described entrepreneurship as 'the Holy Grail of the free enterprise system' — would that this was true. Maybe it is. There's nothing that says the Holy Grail must be shared. There will always be a greedy side to humanity that believes that 'once I've made it, anyone else who hasn't had the same chance will have to find their own way.' The school of hard knocks is much more appealing after you succeed. Hard work should not be confused with hard knocks. Success requires real effort and a broad approach, much of which we've discussed here. Whatever we can do to open the path for others and give them the opportunity to do that hard work and reach their potential will benefit society."

I suppose Sam wanted to add a little gravity to the day. There is no official status or designation that confirms a person as an entrepreneur. Recognition comes through achievement, but a wide range of individual success that benefits society goes unnoticed. The glory of entrepreneurship, if there is such a thing, accrues to the ultra-successful, not to the millions around the world making things happen on a small scale every day. The latter constitute the economic engine that Sam was so preoccupied in unleashing. That was a major part of his message that day.

"For me, entrepreneurship is an instrument, a talent, a catalyst, the resource that frees up all other resources. It offers a universal better lifestyle to those who have the talent, as well as to all in society who can benefit from that talent. Free enterprise celebrates the genius of entrepreneurs, but it does not unleash their genuine collective power. Instead of removing barriers we celebrate those that overcome them. Governments welcome the results achieved by entrepreneurs relying heavily on them to perform in tough times to stimulate the private sector, but do not encourage or welcome entrepreneurship within the bureaucracy. At the moment, there is far more talent suppressed around the world than there is performing and creating jobs and opportunity. So many people have ability that they don't get the chance to use. It will be up to government to break the bonds of ignorance through education to reveal hidden aptitudes and untapped capacity. Education in general, but also programs focused specifically on fostering entrepreneurs. This idea is not about domination by free enterprise. It's about using a key resource to benefit society in more than one way.

"Adam Smith recognized the power of a 'nation of shop-keepers' preoccupied with trade and commerce to influence government and eventually build the most powerful nation in the world, an empire upon which the sun did not set. The outgrowth of that empire has been a relatively enlightened commonwealth. A group of nations that promotes many of the solutions we need to pursue in order to free up entrepreneurial power including education, more welcoming cultural values, and multiculturalism itself. Frankly the commonwealth has merely scratched the surface regarding what can be done and what the ultimate benefits can be. A true global economy will continue to find ways to greater freedom and more widespread benefits to society derived from entrepreneurial ability. I expect all of you to be one of the modern 'shopkeepers' who perform individually, but also lobby governments to remove the barriers that exist around the world, including right here."

One aspect that Sam did not dwell on about his "tribe" was constant thinking, which he demonstrated daily. Sam never stopped thinking or analyzing. His mind was always probing for a better way, whether in business, in economics, in politics, or just in life. It was a relentless crusade, literally the road to continuous improvement, and he was dragging us along with him.

"Right now we are living in a false economy. We have been for a long while. The enlargement of every component of society is not in our best interests. Bigger is not always better. In business and in government, the behemoths our society has created ignore the law of diminishing returns and overemphasize the benefits of economies of scale. We have moved way past the optimum size of operation in many areas. The whole idea of 'too big to fail,' which we've been hearing so much about this year, means we choose to subsidize failure and encourage reckless behaviour. Small business is never given nor can it afford such a miscarriage of economic principle. If fear of failure is a powerful motivation to work hard, make things happen, take chances, and succeed, how do we damage ourselves if we remove failing as a possibility?

"In the west we've created a bubble by ignoring basic business judgement, lending money to people who were not qualified and who would not be able to pay it back at artificially low interest rates in order to sustain a real estate market and an economy past the point of the need for a downturn. This suited the politicians because it distracted the public from the waste of foreign wars that were ineffective and costly. Recessions and depressions happen for a reason. They are corrections to redirect society back on to a sustainable economic path. When we short circuit them by actions such as 'too big to fail,' we mask the symptoms and allow the disease to spread. I want you to understand this because you must head into this false economy as independent business people with your eyes open.

"Ask the labourer in China who lives in a dormitory nine months a year across the road from the factory he works in if we are engaged in a false economy. We live in a world of compromised values. The most dynamic nation in the world, focused on free enterprise, has for its largest trading partner and major debtor the foremost communist nation. Why? So we can sustain this same false economy by providing cheap merchandise to the developed world on the backs of those labourers living away from home in those dormitories. How false are things? How long can nations that have run up excessive debt continue to print money, borrow from themselves, and keep interest rates at ridiculously low levels when their credit worthiness is in question? Don't rely on China as the saviour of the world economy. The Chinese have studied the success of economic imperialism — far more cost effective and lasting than military domination. They are following the example we have laid out over the past century. We are approaching a critical tipping point and we need to take a step back from the abyss.

"Yet, we are in unchartered waters. Our leaders are unsure, making up new economic rules and guidelines as they wing their way through, trying to avoid corrections that need to happen. The longer we postpone the pain, the more severe we will feel the impact. China-proof your business so it cannot be ripped from your grasp and moderate your risk by building a downside plan that does not depend on the growth of our economy, even allowing for shrinkage and continued recession on and off for the next ten years. Does this make me anti-government? Absolutely not! I am a Keynesian. I believe that government has to correct the excessiveness of individualism, which is the basis of our false economy, just as free enterprise has to correct the excessiveness of government by seeking efficiency within the bureaucracy. Regardless, government intervention takes a bad rap.

"The concept of collective intervention has been around for a long time. Do you remember the story in the bible of Joseph in Egypt and his interpretation of Pharaoh's dreams, which so endeared him to the Egyptians? This goes back quite a way in the wisdom of mankind. The logic is fundamental. There will always be good years and bad; sometimes there will be extended cycles of both, say seven years. In the good years collectively, which means through government, we must horde or save for the bad times, and during the bad times we must distribute these savings so that society can survive and people can live. Keynes relied in government to do exactly that. Governments are to run surpluses in good times. The economy does not need help when things are booming. In bad times governments need to spend some of that surplus or inject stimulus to help society rebound and be ready for the next series of good years. It is a cycle, one we've all heard about, the business cycle, which left to its own devices (greed and fear) will have periods of excessive boom and extreme bust. Does it not make sense to balance the budget over a clear economic time frame such as the business cycle as opposed to an arbitrary period like a year or a political term, neither of which is in phase with business conditions?

"During our lifetime, governments around the world have been irresponsible, running deficits in good times, compromising their ability to stimulate in bad times, like right now. In my opinion we have no choice. We have to deal with recession and potential depression now while also putting in place plans for the medium term that will reduce debt and bring new efficiencies to government.

"The irony is that if we cut funding for education, health care, and foreign aid, we will be limiting the release of entrepreneurial talent around the world even more and restricting our future. Free enterprise and government have to end their feud and recognize that they badly need each other. The goals of government need to be revisited focused by the shopkeepers around the world, not by so-called business leaders, heads of huge entities, which have lost touch with reality. At the same time, the excesses of individualism, which can shackle new entrepreneurship, need to be curtailed. I just want you to understand that we are in a period of uncertainty. You can and will succeed within it, but only if you understand what's going on. I'm far from positive that I do."

Finally he reached for his bottle of water. His message was sinking in. Control the things that you can and plan for the things that you can't.

"That's enough about the macro world outside our domain. Let's focus on your future. I stand before you an accidental entrepreneur — exactly what you wanted to hear after two weeks of listening to me rave on about the joys and responsibility of entrepreneurship. If Robin's father had lived longer I would have been an academic, far removed from the business world that I've come to love. There are many of us that don't recognize our entrepreneurial ability until its thrust upon us. Somehow you have found your way to the world of business either by necessity or by opportunity; it doesn't matter which. Your straightjackets have been removed and you are ready to launch. Tough times often bring out the best in us. I wish you only success. As the Irish say, 'may you live as long as you want, and never want as long as you live.'"

The applause was loud; way beyond what you might have expected from the three doubting novices who had first met there two weeks before. I had been designated to thank Sam.

"It's said that every once in a while you meet someone that has a profound effect on your life. I've been waiting for that to happen, and this week it has."

Sam laughed along with everyone else.

"Robin called you an enigma, so I looked that up. The word means 'a person or a thing that is mysterious, puzzling or hard to understand.' Well Sam, you started off mysterious and you are certainly still puzzling, but I don't find you hard to understand. I hope that we can contact you occasionally for advice, but you have covered a tremendous amount of ground that is going to help all of us in the years ahead. To just say thank you seems inadequate, but there are no better words. Thank you so much. We'll try and make you proud and help in some small way in your crusade to free every potential entrepreneur to do what *we* can do best."

Sam noticed the emphasis on "we" which brought a smile to his face, but he wasn't quite finished. Behind his desk were three packages wrapped in plain brown paper. Without comment, he handed out the designated one with our name on it to each of us. Grace and I accepted ours without opening them. There was no way that Mike was that patient. His paper was ripped off in seconds to reveal a very nicely framed certificate, quite official looking, seal and all, that stated: "Mike Reynolds has faithfully attended my seminar program on Entrepreneurship." That was it. Not the ringing endorsement I was looking for, but this was just an informal two week course at the summer cottage, even if it seemed like more. Attached to the certificate, below the statement was a crisp new five dollar bill under which was written. "If things don't work out, there's always coffee and donuts at the Deli-Caf."

Mike was elated. I'm not sure he had any certificates that he could hang on a wall. He shook hands with Sam enthusiastically, ready to get on his way.

Sam had one last word for him.

"Mike, you've surprised me. Maybe you'd like to sit in on my next class. I hear you have the afternoons free?"

Mike was beaming. He'd been convinced that Sam didn't like him.

"I'd really like that, Sam. I do have one confession to make. There is one thing I definitely learned here; if it's only about the money, it's not going to happen."

Then he rushed out to show his certificate to Terry and Jen.

Sam was laughing out loud as he turned back to find Grace and I still sitting at our desks.

"I know what you call me. I work hard to ensure that from the first day on I'm known as 'The Everyday Entrepreneur.' I do it on purpose. It's a term I want deeply imbedded in your psyche by the time you leave here for good. Oh, it does refer to me. I am one of the unknown, who relish the challenge, accept the risk and do our best. But for the purpose of our little exercise 'The Everyday Entrepreneur' is my name for all of you, every one of you who passes through these doors on your way to your own business. I only wish I could help more people along the way."

So we left the school that day with a new designation — everyday entrepreneurs. No letters to add behind our name, but we had captured a distinct confidence that we were not alone. It was no surprise that Sam would have the last laugh. Hugs and handshakes were happily exchanged. It was a good day.

CHAPTER TWENTY-SIX

One Last Surprise

On the way to the Deli-Caf, Grace and I put the unwrapped certificates in our cars. Neither of us we're in a hurry to go home. By the time we walked inside Mike had already left, eager to show his mom his new credentials and to get a good night's sleep, since he was committed to meet Jen at three in the morning.

Terry and Jen were beaming. The new Mike had that effect on people. There was no one else there. Sunday wound up early in the midst of the prime season. Jen looked tired. She had been pushing the envelope the last few days, starting at three each morning and hanging around for us to finish every afternoon. She and Grace hugged while Terry and I shook hands as I thanked him.

"You were right. Sam sure changed my outlook. I'm anxious to get started."

Grace was more emotional, crying as she still held on to Jen.

"Your parents are great. I mean, I'm sure they could be tough as parents, but they've got such a great philosophy of life. It's contagious. That was quite a speech Sam made today. He should be a politician."

Jen laughed.

"Don't encourage him. My mom's been chastising him for lecturing since I can remember, especially at dinner parties. But he does have different insight and he's never dull."

We all agreed on that. Sam was not dull. Terry made an interesting point.

"I'm surprised that he invited Mike back. He usually has nothing good to say about the 'one in three' guy other than good riddance. That's one relationship he can't wait to end. Mike must have wedged his way into his heart somehow. Although, I wondered when he gave him the five bucks with his certificate; that's generally the brush off."

I had wondered about that as well. The fallback to coffee at the Deli-Caf seemed a little rough for all of us. I assumed my reward would be the same. I'm not sure why, but I felt the need to defend Mike.

"Mike still has a lot to learn. I thought it was great that Sam invited him back. Mike was different the last few days. Maybe he faced some of his demons and came away laughing at them. Maybe he saw a little of his father in Sam. It sounds like his dad was the same kind of guy. Whatever the reason, his time with Sam changed him. It's up to you to keep the momentum."

Terry nodded.

"I remember his dad now. Maybe you do to. We used to pick up his garbage. Remember the big place out on Bass Island? I just put it together when Mike was in here today. The guy that gave us the water ski lessons that summer as well as the twenty dollar tip each, that was Mike's father. I should have recognized his mother. She was a blond then; we thought she was pretty hot. He was probably our best customer and he was great on the skis. Remember how sharp he could cut on the slalom course he put in out there? You and I used to run that course every day. I hope we're better as Everyday Entrepreneurs."

All four of us laughed at that. Terry had always been a bit of a scamp.

"You knew about that all the time. I think you even planted the name on the first day we all came in here."

Anyway, things had come full circle. Mr. Reynolds had been

kind to us. Now his son was skiing barefoot and showing us up, but more important we could return the kindness after all these years. I wished I had remembered earlier so I could have told Mike. I hoped the chance would come.

Jen said. "We have something for the two of you. Have you opened your packages from Sam yet? You can't see our surprise until you do."

It was getting late so I went out to the cars to retrieve both packages. As I did the happy banter continued. When I got back I handed Grace her package. I wanted her to open hers first in case mine was a disappointment. She ripped off the paper almost as fast as Mike had. Her eyes lit up immediately when she saw what was inside. I couldn't see because the back of the certificate was facing me until she turned it around. Where Mike had received a five dollar bill, Grace had a brand new crisp one hundred dollar bill. There were actually ten of them, but only one was attached. The certificate read: "Grace Freeman has completed my seminar on entrepreneurship and has attained the status of 'Everyday Entrepreneur.'" Below the hundred dollar bill was written: "All entrepreneurs need seed capital. I am pleased to be the first to send you on the road to success. But I expect you to help other new entrepreneurs after you succeed." It was signed simply "Sam Macleod."

Now I was sure that I shouldn't open mine. A thousand dollars; Sam was full of surprises. I had seen the two extremes, what variation would he have given me? Probably nothing. I really didn't need anything but Grace did.

Grace was overwhelmed. "Oh my, that's much too generous. But it will certainly help out. I can do the whole back office for Doug with this. C'mon, Tim, open yours."

I really was afraid. Sure I would be embarrassed, but what choice did I have? As it turned out there was nothing to worry about. My certificate was exactly the same as the one Grace had, one thousand dollars and all, except the name was changed to

Tim Davidson and there was a small hand written note attached on a post-it. I didn't show the note to any of them. It said "Thanks for showing up this summer. Terry has found himself since you got here. I think it helped him figure things out with Jen. Don't be a stranger. Sam."

No chance of that. I planned to spend more time at the cottage. But the note brought another surprise. I had no idea that Terry had been down. He had been his old self the whole time as far as I could see. I thought that I was the one who was dejected when I arrived.

Jen couldn't wait any longer. She handed both of us envelopes with what looked like cards. Her excitement was contagious.

"Okay, open them at the same time. Go!"

Inside was the last surprise of the day, identical cards of congratulations and five crisp new hundred dollar bills for each of us. That was too much. Jen and Terry didn't think it was enough.

"You're our first new entrepreneurs. We're not quite living up to Sam's challenge, but it's a new start for all of us. We wanted to help both of you get started."

I could only hope to do that much for someone else.

EPILOGUE

June 28, 2013

Four years have passed since that valediction day. Sam was right to have warned us about the economy. The only certainty continues to be uncertainty. Champions of large government and unfettered free enterprise remain uncompromised in what seems like a death struggle to undermine the foundation of the other. No one in a position of power around the world has adopted Sam's premise that they are irrevocably linked, each needing the other to maximize their potential. Without government action, immeasurable entrepreneurial capacity will continue to be unreachable. Without the impact of increased entrepreneurial talent within government, the focus of our collective will, manifested in our institutions, must continue to languish in bureaucracy and inefficiency.

It does seem that all of us who came together that summer have picked our niche markets well. Most businesses succeeding in these troubled times have placed a heavy weight on cost control and cost reduction. Even so, my former employer did not make it easy for me to resign. When I presented my resignation along with a detailed proposal for a contract to replace their existing training program with an interactive online seminar program of my design, their first reaction was to claim that the idea was proprietary, having been developed while I was in their employ. My new lawyer, a young hawk at a national legal firm in a prestigious downtown office, was ready for that.

We presented several other parallel programs, which I had thrown together at his direction, with completely different applications using many of the same techniques contemplated for in-house training for a whole range of unrelated products and services, as well as those of my employer. There was no doubt that my system had a wide range of applications completely unconnected to my existing role. Their initial indignity morphed itself quickly into a new offer of a promotion and a large raise. When this attractive offer was politely declined, we negotiated a better contract than I had expected, primarily because they had shown their hand, making me better prepared, more willing to be firm and able to negotiate from strength. If I hadn't met Sam I would have taken their offer without countering, or more likely I would never have made mine and would still be a mid-level employee.

A further outgrowth of that negotiating ploy was that I was able to parlay some of those hastily conceived programs into serious opportunities, initially with other clients of the law firm. Online Studies Inc., has business, education, and entertainment divisions. The website and the teaching program are common to all three and are exceptionally interactive, which was one of my principal goals. The web designer was Doug Freeman. His company now has a six figure annual contract to maintain and refine the website.

We located the head office in Waterloo, tapping into the abundant pool of talent attracted there by RIM as well as streaming out of the universities. We have also recruited heavily from the retired professors in the area to run full-scale programs in their specialties and to have others show up as guest speakers in various seminar series. This group is the foundation of our education department. The focus has been primarily on business, economics, and computer science. Our timing has been excellent since retraining, and upgrading skills have become priorities during the economic downturn. The education division is headed up by an MBA graduate that I hired two years ago. You may remember Jennifer Kelly. The hours at the Deli-Caf proved to be too much, so Jen decided to find something more conventional, related to her education. Her RIM contacts have been invaluable for recruiting staff and contractors alike.

Specialized business seminars have flourished for the same reason. We've been able to run joint programs with national associations of realtors, accountants, and retailers. The associations provide the content which we integrate into our delivery system. All of these programs are very targeted and can be implemented for national associations or catered to companies with multiple locations. The cost effectiveness of online access has been tremendous. More and more firms are setting up training rooms, saving travel costs and time while providing training on a convenient and cost-effective basis right in their office space. The most essential element is the interactive nature of the system, which allows for immediate feedback in combination with the opportunity to revisit the original seminar during the week it's presented. During that week we also offer three review tutorials, which are interactive sessions focused on questions and answers as opposed to presenting any new material. As you might expect, I spend most of my time focused on this department.

We've had less success with our personal entertainment division — there's simply too much competition. Last year we moved away from the mainstream areas of interactive home entertainment, such as how to write a blog, how to produce your own music, how to build a family website, and so on, shifting towards arts and crafts, more basic and traditional areas with a large potential audience. Once again, it's the interactive element that attracts people. We can also attract a large audience, which gives us the opportunity to bring in specialists that may otherwise be unreachable for many subscribers.

Unfortunately our Blend a Good Yarn seminar series with Grace Freeman had to be cancelled. Grace simply didn't have the time to continue. She now has six stores in the metropolitan area and is looking at franchising them across the country. She writes a very successful blog with many advertisers and a huge following of knitters. Her ability to combine traditional hobbies with computer-generated patterns and communication has been dynamic, helping to revitalize a waning form of creativity that is satisfying and relaxing.

I forgot to mention that Terry is also out of the Deli-Caf, back into real estate as an independent broker, including a second office in cottage country. You see, he still has to be there because he and Jen have their own cottage now. Last year they bought one third of Bass Island. Also, he can't let his other partner down. That's right. Mike now owns 50 percent of the Deli-Caf, which he operates seasonally from May to the end of August, leaving him time for his winter job *and* to go to school. Mike is taking his MBA. I wish that I had. And what do you think his winter job is? Well Mike is still acting out the role of the "one in three" guy in our most successful seminar series called "The Everyday Entrepreneur." Like all our seminars, that one is interactive, but the lecturer still insists on having three people live in his class-room. At least one must be a woman, and then there's Mike, acting out a role that once came so naturally for which he now understands the importance. I don't remember the "one in three" guy being quite that dramatic in that first session, but he plays the part very well. It doesn't seem to matter who the other party is, which gives me pause to wonder how being the third wheel affected me so dramatically four years ago.

All of us have made good on the challenge to financially help new entrepreneurs, several times over. As for Sam, the seminars have greatly expanded his audience and his reach. He's still on that crusade to free up all the unfulfilled entrepreneurial ability that exists in this world. Sam has founded a new organization with chapters growing worldwide called the World Economic Society of Everyday Entrepreneurs (WESEE).

This is the Thursday before the long weekend. Time to get to the cottage; all of us will be there at the Deli-Caf. I can hardly wait.

APPENDIX I

Sam Says:

1. It's not about the money.
2. Entrepreneurs are born, but they can also be made, developed, and nurtured.
3. Underestimating the competition is a reckless and unnecessary risk.
4. Indecision almost always leads to bad decisions.
5. The question must never be if a thing *can* be done but rather how it *will* be done.
6. Face the things you like least and find a way to do them.
7. What? Look for the opportunity when it arises, *not* when you need it.
8. Opportunities are not the mirror image of ideas.
9. Ask questions! Ask questions! Ask questions!
10. Entrepreneurship is a philosophy based on action.
11. The stability of government and society is critical for upward mobility.
12. Economics is a behavioural science. Fear and greed are the dominant emotions.
13. Greed leads to boom then bubble. Fear leads to bust.
14. One of the biggest reasons for small business failure is daydreaming at the start.

15. Don't confuse the perceptive nature of true genius with unattainable dreams.
16. Opportunities must be worthwhile and viable — forget the whimsical.
17. Rigidity in the banking systems is severely limiting small business.
18. Ground your business plan in reality. Take the emotion out of your thought process.
19. Pay yourself! Pay yourself! Pay yourself!
20. Commitment is one of the foundations of success.
21. The most dangerous person who can fool you about your own business is you.
22. Strive for success, defend against failure.
23. Things can go wrong, so negotiate to cover the downside.
24. There are no guarantees. Do your homework first, then trust your instincts.
25. When things do go wrong, the ability to adjust is your lifeline.
26. Never make a decision on the premise "I can stand the loss."
27. There is no such thing as entrepreneurial infallibility.
28. When you incur a tax loss, remember the word "tax" is just an adjective.
29. Never be satisfied with failure as the end game.
30. Small business is part of the global economy, not a junior subset.
31. There will always be voids in the marketplace.
32. The global economy embodies change, which mandates flexibility.
33. Structural unemployment is best solved by entrepreneurs with a local bias.
34. Cultivate relationships in India and with likeminded entrepreneurs elsewhere.
35. No entrepreneur worth his salt is immune to self-doubt.
36. Free enterprise needs government to ensure opportunity.

37. Government needs the drive and efficiency of free enterprise to stay viable.
38. Countries, like any other entity, cannot be sustained by debt indefinitely.
39. Entrepreneurship of necessity is very different from entrepreneurship of opportunity.
40. Entrepreneurs of any stripe make things happen!
41. Entrepreneurs are agents of change — the principal catalysts of economic progress.
42. Overall, your business has to be fun. You have to like what you do.
43. Things that you don't like still have to be done, and on time!
44. Everything cannot be simple. Sometimes you have to study to understand.
45. Every problem is an opportunity.
46. Decisions must be delivered with authority, not uncertainty.
47. Don't confuse inventors or investors with entrepreneurs.
48. Know and understand your numbers.
49. Cash flow never lies.
50. Where expenditures are concerned: Payback rules!
51. Don't let your enthusiasm lead to commitments that make you vulnerable
52. *Ass*ume makes an "ass" of "u" and "me."
53. One set of assumptions is reckless.
54. There is no such thing as planning with certainty.
55. Projects can take twice as long, cost twice as much, and make half the profits we plan.
56. Make realism temper your enthusiasm, but don't lose your drive as a result.
57. Negotiation is a process that has to evolve.
58. Never enter into negotiation without being prepared. Understand the other side.
59. You can learn as much from your failures as from your success.

60. Most partnerships don't end well.

61. Merging business with family can work, but it can also compromise both.

62. Partners seldom agree how a business evolved or who made what contribution.

63. Salesmen are like halfbacks, getting the glory, but going nowhere without the team.

64. Relationships take work.

65. Creativity is the cornerstone of shameless self-promotion.

66. Never forget to ask for the order.

67. One good supplier can help you succeed with hundreds of good customers.

68. Relationships, creativity, and innovation are integrated and interdependent.

69. The electronic revolution levels the playing field for independent entrepreneurs.

70. Don't lose balance! Don't lose balance! Don't lose balance!

71. You have to work to live. There is no meaningful future in living to work.

72. Beware hyper connectivity — 24/7 is a recipe for disaster.

73. Don't make your business too big. It benefits everyone but you.

74. Don't let your business outgrow you.

75. Remember the crocodile farm — beware commitments that eat up your profits.

76. Entrepreneurs are self-starters.

77. There are people that make things happen, others who watch things happen, and many who wonder what happened.

78. Remember the "nation of shopkeepers" that built an empire.

79. You are a generalist, wearing every hat possible.

80. What you do pay yourself must be fair to you and your company.

81. Fair pay includes at least 10 percent that must be saved.

82. Income splitting is a right. Don't abuse it, but make sure you use it.

83. Keep your personal investments separate from your business. Balance.
84. Your business is not you.
85. Invest in yourself — seminars, trade shows. Payback is in your hands and your ideas.
86. Take vacations! Take vacations! Take vacations!
87. Be decisive — leaders are.
88. Develop pride of performance, not of position.
89. Be determined — leaders are.
90. Don't underestimate the power of confidence. Don't undermine it with ego.
91. Motivation — the fear of failure or the drive for success?
92. Greed leads to bad decisions.
93. You only pay tax if you make the money.
94. Never forget the inverse relationship between risk and reward.
95. Remember "Freedom 95."
96. Do you understand the meaning of "unlimited liability?"
97. Most entrepreneurial skills and experiences are transferable to new opportunities.
98. Don't go cheap on legal and accounting advice.
99. Like it or not, you do need a banker.
100. We live in a false economy.
101. "Too big to fail" subsidizes failure and encourages reckless behaviour.
102. We are in uncharted political and economic waters, featuring a crisis of leadership.
103. China-proof your business.
104. Don't build your plan based on growth/economic recovery — that's the upside.
105. Control the things you can and allow for the things you can't.

APPENDIX II

The Vaunted Curve

Sam's Theory

1. Everyone has some element of entrepreneurial skills, from zero to hero.
2. The percentage of the population with each skill level can be plotted on to a normal distribution represented by a bell curve.
3. The peak of the curve is the average skill level — 50 percent of the population is on each side.
4. Those on the left side possess less than average entrepreneurial aptitude.
5. Those on the extreme left have virtually no such skills.
6. Those on the right side possess more than average entrepreneurial aptitude.
7. Those on the extreme right possess the genius we celebrate, from Edison to Jobs.
8. The application of these skills is thwarted by a wide range of obstacles.
9. The world economy is only utilizing a small percentage of the total entrepreneurial skills available due to the limitations of culture, education, gender bias, etc.
10. Governments are the key to removing these barriers over time.

11. Government tends to be staffed by people on the left side. There needs to be a shift.

12. Those that fall on the right side of the curve are the key to solving localized economic problems, particularly structural employments issues and job creation, whereas big business will look elsewhere, pursuing competitive advantages that aren't available to small independent business.

One of the main reasons to accept Sam's premise is the North American experience. We still have many barriers here. Maybe they're not as severe as they once were, but there is still too much talent denied opportunity. However, it's no accident that there has been a parade of people here from other countries over the past two hundred years. Major cultural and social issues have been recognized here and at least partially dealt with, opening up opportunities not available elsewhere. Sam is right, the more we remove these limitations, the more that can be accomplished through the efforts of entrepreneurs working in concert with a government determined to provide essential services on an efficient basis. We are the experiment that proves the conclusion. Entrepreneurship thrives here like nowhere else. However, the reduction of obstacles that has happened here has been largely accomplished at the hands of an inefficient government. There is more to be done on all fronts. The experiment is still in progress. Entrepreneurship can only achieve optimum results in a free and stable society. Government is the only institution that can guarantee that freedom and provide the stability and infrastructure required for that success. To do this on an affordable, sustainable basis government has to adopt practices from the private sector.

APPENDIX III

1. "Ain't No Mountain High Enough" — Diana Ross
2. "On a Clear Day (You Can See Forever)" — Barbra Streisand
3. "Imagine" — John Lennon
4. "I Dreamed a Dream" — Susan Boyle
5. "Somewhere Over the Rainbow" — Israel Kamakawiwo'ole
6. "I Believe" — Nikki Yanofsky
7. "What a Wonderful World" — Louis Armstrong
8. "This Is the Moment" — Colm Wilkinson
9. "Don't Rain on My Parade" — Barbra Streisand
10. "We Will Rock You" — Queen
11. "Circle of Life" — Broadway Cast of the Lion King
12. "One More Day" — London Cast of Les Miserables
13. "We Are the Champions" — Queen
14. "Eye of the Tiger" — Survivor
15. "The Wonder of You" — Elvis Presley

No surprise, most of these are positive, even inspiring. When you're feeling down or frustrated, give the list a try. Sam chose the last one for Robin, who keeps him balanced, and his good friend Ken, the thought of whom will always remind Sam that a playlist is never complete without at least one song by Elvis.

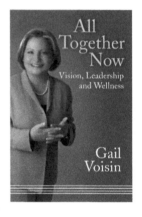